The Year of the Poet V

December 2018

The Poetry Posse

inner child press, ltd.

The Poetry Posse 2018

Gail Weston Shazor

Shareef Abdur Rasheed

Teresa E. Gallion

hülya n. yılmaz

Kimberly Burnham

Tzemin Ition Tsai

Elizabeth Esguerra Castillo

Jackie Davis Allen

Nizar Sartawi

Caroline 'Ceri' Nazareno

Ashok K. Bhargava

Alicja Maria Kuberska

Swapna Behera

William S. Peters, Sr.

General Information

The Year of the Poet V

December 2018 Edition
Series # 60

The Poetry Posse

1st Edition : 2018

Publisher Information

1st Edition : Inner Child Press
intouch@innerchildpress.com
www.innerchildpress.com

ISBN-13 : 978-1-970020-68-7 (inner child press, ltd.)

$ 12.99

WHAT WOULD LIFE BE WITHOUT A LITTLE POETRY?

Dedication

This Book is dedicated to

Poetry . . .

The Poetry Posse

past, present & future

our Patrons and Readers

the Spirit of our Everlasting Muse

&

the Power of the Pen

to effectuate change!

In the darkness of my life
I heard the music
I danced . . .
and the Light appeared
and I dance

Janet P. Caldwell

Janet Perkins Caldwell

Rest In Peace

February 14, 1959 ~ September 20, 2016

Rest In Peace Dear Brother

Alan W. Jankowski

16 March 1961 ~ 10 March 2017

Poets . . .
sowing seeds in the
Conscious Garden of Life,
that those who have yet to come
may enjoy the Flowers.

Table of Contents

The Poetry Posse

Table of Contents . . . *continued*

Foreword

The Māori are the indigenous Polynesian people of New Zealand. Māori originated with settlers from eastern Polynesia, who arrived in New Zealand in several waves of canoe voyages between 1250 and 1300. Most archaeologists and historians believe that the Maori people came from the Cook Islands and the Polynesian region. Some scholars believe that the origin of the Maori people and all the South Island languages can be traced back to Taiwan in the western Pacific. The language, culture and traditional architecture of the Maori people are very similar to the Ami people in Taiwan. This provides very clear evidence

Over several centuries in isolation, the Polynesian settlers developed a unique culture, with their own language, a rich mythology, and distinctive crafts and performing arts. Early Māori formed tribal groups based on eastern Polynesian social customs and organisation.

Before the arrival of British immigrants at the end of the 18th century, Maori were mainly engaged in agriculture, fishing, hunting and gathering. Now Maori culture is the national culture of New Zealand. It is reflected in tattoos, war dance and folk art. They are good at carving and weaving. Among them, carvings include wood carvings and stone carvings. They are the essence of Maori art.

Researchers often label the time from about 1280 to about 1450 the "Moa-hunter period" - after the moa, the large flightless bird that formed a large part of the diet of the early settlers. In the early days, only some islanders went to Otto Rova to find and hunt for Moa birds. They ignited the forest while hunting, so when the Moa birds discovered New Zealand a few hundred years later, the Moa birds have long since disappeared.

In 1280, seven canoes came to Otto Rova from the island countries of the South Pacific. This is the first planned islander immigration. During the two hundred years, the Maori lived in the North Island of New Zealand and the South Island.

In the fourteenth century, the Maori people living in the South Pacific opened up the history of New Zealand civilization. For centuries they have developed a rigorous tribal system, class system, and highly accomplished artistic representation. Before the arrival of Western civilization, Maori people have always lived in their traditional social form.

In addition to the ethnic minorities that have been oppressed or assimilated in many other countries, Maori have more say in New Zealand and their culture is more well preserved. The language of the country is recognized by the laws of New Zealand. Even so, Maori is still at risk of being marginalized by New Zealand's white mainstream society, as less than half of Maori use Maori in their daily lives, and many Maori can do not fluently speak Maori nowadays.

Tzemin Ition Tsai

Poets, Writers . . . know that we are the enchanting magicians that nourishes the seeds of dreams and thoughts . . . it is our words that entice the hearts and minds of others to believe there is something grand about the possibilities that life has to offer and our words tease it forth into action . . . for you are the Poet, the Writer to whom the Gift of Words has been entrusted . . .

~ wsp

Preface

Dear Family and Friends,

Congratualtions to all the Poetry Posse Members … past and present!

Yes I am excited? Once again, this is an understatement! As we are hitting another milestone, the final issue of our fifth year of publication . . . I am elated.

Our initial vision was to just perform at this level for the year of 2014. Since that time we have had the blessed opportunity to include many other wonderful word artists and storytellers in the Poetry Posse from lands, cultures and persuasions all over the world. We have featured hundreds of additional poets, thereby introducing their poetic offerings to our vast global readership.

In keeping with our effort and vision to expand the awareness of poets from all walks by making this offerings accessible, we at Inner Child Press will continue to make every volume a FREE Download. The books are also available for purchase at the affordable cost of $7.00 per volume.

In the previous years, our monthly themes were Flowers, Birds, Gemstones and Trees. This year we have elected to take a different direction by theming our offerings after *Cultures* of past and present. In each month's volume you will have the opportunity to not only read at least one poem themed by our Poetry Posse members about such culture, but we have included a few words about the culture in our prologue. The reasoning behind this is that now our poetry has the opportunity to be educational for not only the reader, but we poets as well. We hope you find the poetic offerings insightful as we use our poetic form to relay to you what we too have learned through our research in making our offering available to you, our readership.

Going into the year 2019 we will again theme our efforts to encompass various world cultures as defined by their language and geography. We are following the model of UNESCO and their mission of educational inclusiveness.

In closing, we would like to thank you for being an integral part of our amazing journey.

Enjoy our amazing featured poets . . . they are amazing!

Inner Child Press International

'building cultural bridges of understanding'

Bless Up

From our house to yours

Bill

The Poetry Posse
Inner Child Press

PS

Do Not forget about the World Healing, World Peace Poetry effort.

Available here

www.worldhealingworldpeacepoetry.com

or

Janet . . . gone too soon.

http://www.innerchildpress.com/janet-p-caldwell.php

For Free Downloads of Previous Issues of The Year of the Poet

www.innerchildpress.com/the-year-of-the-poet

poetry is . . .
India INK

The Maori

The Maori are a people who hail originally from New Zealand. They are the indigenous Polynesians. The Maori people spent several centuries in isolation. With the arrival of the European people some time in the 17th century, the people were colonized and soon began adoption the "Western" ways. The European having invaded their lands began to want more. The Maori entered the Treaty of Waitangi February 6, 1840 in good faith hoping to bring peace to the lands and their people. As treaties go throughout the days of European global colonization, it was broken, and the people suffered even more under the oppressive hand. For the most part, the Maori people were able to hold on to their unique culture as many migrated away from their indigenous homelands to various islands throughout the South Pacific.

For more information visit :

https://en.wikipedia.org/wiki/M%C4%81ori_people

https://intercontinentalcry.org/indigenous-peoples/maori/

https://www.newzealand.com/us/maori-culture/

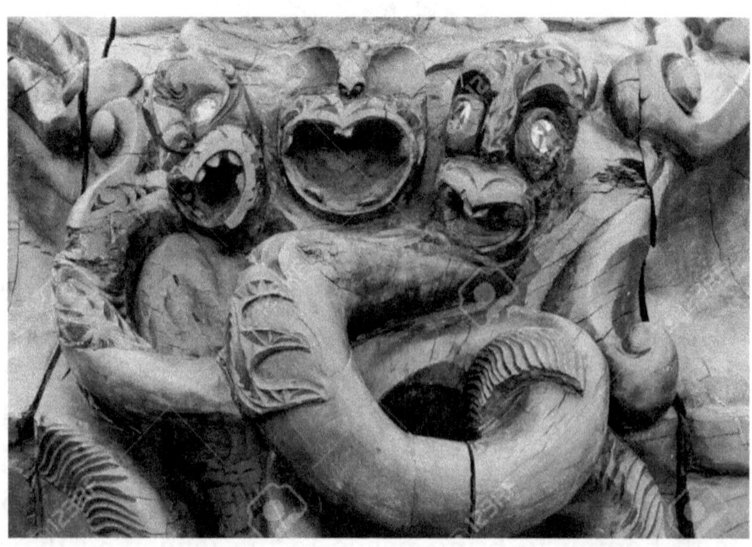

The Year of the Poet V

December 2018

The Poetry Posse

inner child press, ltd.

Poetry succeeds where instruction fails.

~ wsp

Gail

Weston

Shazor

This is a creative promise ~ my pen will speak to and for the world. Enamored with letters and respectful of their power, I have been writing for most of my life. A mother, daughter, sister and grandmother I give what I have been given, greatfilledly.

Author of . . .

"An Overstanding of an Imperfect Love"
&
Notes from the Blue Roof

Lies My Grandfathers Told Me

available at Inner Child Press.

www.facebook.com/gailwestonshazor
www.innerchildpress.com/gail-weston-shazor
navypoet1@gmail.com

Ka Mate Haka

Ka mate, ka mate! ka ora! ka ora!
Ka mate! ka mate! ka ora! ka ora!
Tēnei te tangata pūhuruhuru
Nāna nei i tiki mai whakawhiti te rā
Ā, upane! ka upane!
Ā, upane, ka upane, whiti te ra!

Te Rauparaha faced the black walls
Of an even blacker pit
And his soul sang
Ka mate, ka mate!
I hide myself in here
This is my cleft of refuge
Though the enemy chases me
I am safe

ka ora! ka ora!

I will live til the rising of the sun
I will meet the warmth
Of friendly kinsmen

Ā, upane! ka upane!

Upward from the darkness
I will rise the same

whiti te ra!

And I live to see the day again
For this Man has said so...

Tapes

I want to measure
The strength of you
The height, breadth and weight of you
To know you as i wake
After you have breathed the breath
That I find so difficult to hold
Place the palm of your hand
In my chest
Thread your fingers across my ribs
So that I can exhale
Against your will for me
Whisper my name
And pull the breeze close
For when I forget to draw
It for myself
You are here to remind me
Why I must
Though sometimes it hurts to do so
The simpleness of this one thing
Is echoed in comfort
Ease yourself you say
And your thumbs meditate
The healing in my lungs
It is when you tend to me
That I feel whole

Koinonia

To receive goodness
We must first pour out
All that we have
All that we are
All that they have given us
To make room for the grace
This is the secret
Of living goodness
That the world never shares with us
This is the secret that only family
Can teach us
And even then
Sometimes
Our only heart breaks
In times such as these
It is a hard thing
This living broken

But this, my loves,
Is when the newly formed spaces
Shine brighter than the
Lived through ones

The simple connection
Becomes the necessary
And we have to keep seeking
The strength of each other
And in the broken places
We make room for more
More love
More people

More community
And love is always a sacrifice
And love is always intentional
And living is the love we share
Through all our numbered days
Selah

Alicja
Maria
Kuberska

Alicja Maria Kuberska – awarded Polish poetess, novelist, journalist, editor. She was born in 1960, in Świebodzin, Poland. She now lives in Inowrocław, Poland.
In 2011 she published her first volume of poems entitled: "The Glass Reality". Her second volume "Analysis of Feelings", was published in 2012. The third collection "Moments" was published in English in 2014, both in Poland and in the USA. In 2014, she also published the novel - "Virtual roses" and volume of poems "On the border of dream". Next year her volume entitled "Girl in the Mirror" was published in the UK and "Love me" , " (Not)my poem" in the USA. In 2015 she also edited anthology entitled "The Other Side of the Screen".

In 2016 she edited two volumes: "Taste of Love" (USA), "Thief of Dreams" (Poland) and international anthology entitled " Love is like Air" (USA). In 2017 she published volume entitled "View from the window" (Poland). She also edits series of anthologies entitled "Metaphor of Contemporary" (Poland)

Her poems have been published in numerous anthologies and magazines in Poland, the USA, the UK, Albania, Belgium, Chile, Spain, Israel, Canada, India, Italy, Uzbekistan, Czech Republic, South Korea and Australia. She was a featured poet of New Mirage Journal (USA) in the summer of 2011.

Alicja Kuberska is a member of the Polish Writers Associations in Warsaw, Poland and IWA Bogdani, Albania. She is also a member of directors' board of Soflay Literature Foundation.

Ta moko

Seven boats from Polynesia sailed to the land of a long,
white cloud and moored on a sandy,
sorrunded by rocks, beach.

Finding their paradise on earth, in which they ate kiwi fruit
instead of an apple, they learned the truth about
fertile soil overgrown with majestic jungle.

They saw that the springs of geysers created the island's
bloodstream

A cascade of ice-cold water filled with blue runs down
from the heart of the mountains, too

Echo raised their cries of admiration to the hazy summits:
"Taumatawhakatangihangakoauauotamateaturipukakapiki
maungahoronukupokaiwhenuakitanatahu"

Centuries passed and ancient traditions were stored by
legends and tattoos

Black drawings carved permanent visiting cards on the
faces of the Maori people

The sharp bones of the albatross and dyes wrote a story
about a man on his skin

The winding lines invited the spirits of predecessors and
family sagas on the forehead

They also talked about the wealth and the privileges of his
family, social status and work

The flexible drawings of the right side of the body
were devoted to the mother and the left ones to the father

There are not two identical tattoos, just like there are no
identical fates.

It's amazing how much a man can say without a word

Sometime in Autumn

We walked in the park, hidden under an umbrella
Thick fog imbued us with melancholy,
and cold touched our hands.
Clouds supporting the weight of the rain, hung low over the trees.
Puddles mirrored the reflections of lanterns,
tired by the night vigil.

Suddenly the sun glimmered, and autumn smiled.
Trees discarded grayness, in favor of color.
Droplets of dew sparkled,
and rusty chestnuts danced across the paths.
Yellow leaves, fragrant with moisture, twirled in the breeze.

You spoke quietly of love.
You spun words like threads of Indian Summer.
I committed to memory vibrations of voice
And embrace of clasped fingers.
You held me,
And then you wove an engagement ring out of the grass
-With a white daisy for the diamond

The Next Chance

Carmine roses bloom in the midst of winter,
Drowsy violets peak from under leaves
And daisies stand white in the grass.
The sun heats the earth
And brightens short days with a warm glow.

I notice a tenderly embraced couple in a park.
Gracious fate gives them one more chance
For an unexpected meeting.
Eyes, surrounded by rays of wrinkles, laugh.
Wind ruffles hair, tosses delicate
Silver threads of gossamer.

And so, unannounced, tardy love arrived
They have a choice of a new path,
Maybe the last chance for happiness.
Life took away their naïve faith
And burned away old feelings.
It left them some dreams
And much hope for a better tomorrow

They are lost in thoughts
Doubts and fears spring up
From the shadows like ghouls
The head says: no… it's not worth it… think it over…
The heart says-yes… go forwards… fall in love

Nature stopped the hands of the clocks.
Red flowers bloom

Jackie
Davis
Allen

Jackie Davis Allen, otherwise known as Jacqueline D. Allen or Jackie Allen, grew up in the Cumberland Mountains of Appalachia. As the next eldest daughter of a coal miner father and a stay at home mother, she was the first in her family to attend and graduate from college. Her siblings, in their own right, are accomplished, though she is the only one, to date, that has discovered the gift of writing.

Graduating from Radford University, with a Bachelor of Science degree in ElementaryEducation, she taught in both public and private schools. For over a decade she taught private art classes to children, both in her home and at a local Art and Framing Shop where she also sold her original soft sculptured Victorian dolls and original christening gowns.

She resides in northern Virginia with her husband, taking much needed get-aways to their mountain home near the Blue Ridge Mountains, a place that evokes memories of days spent growing up in the Appalachian Mountains.

A lover of hats, she has worn many. Following marriage to her college sweetheart, and as wife, mother, grandmother, teacher, tutor, artist, writer, poet and crafter, she is a lover of art and antiques, surrounding herself, always, with books, seeking to learn more.

In 2015 she authored *Looking for Rainbows, Poetry, Prose and Art*; in 2017, *Dark Side of the Moon,* and in 2018*, No Illusions-through the looking glass*. Mostly narrative poetry, some prose, memoir and tall tales, published by Inner Child Press, edited by hulya n. yilmaz.

http://www.innerchildpress.com/jackie-davis-allen.php
jackiedavisallen.com

An Introspection

An appreciator of art, sculpture, as in modern, or the New Zealand Maori's, *Whakairo*, wood carvings, a pleasure it would be, to see in person, the art by which a master craftsman handed down their stories and legends; some remaining from over 500 years ago.

Wood was revered. Scraps saved. Not used for cooking. Reminds me of my soft sculpting days: no scrap of fabric, or lace discarded. A use found for it, some day. As always.

A proud possessor, I am, of several rugs: one a Sarouk, and another, a tribal rug. Perhaps a rare Bukhara from Central Asia or Turkey. To stand before a *Ranga*, or to own one, what an experience! Such a weaving, the tapestry upon which the Maori further illustrated their stories and legends, tactilely and visually. Creatively.

The history of the Maori people, they orally improvised as myth-narratives, stories to meet their needs. Laid out before my eyes, to see such a weaving, unforgettable.

A speech maker I am not, but oh, if what I am sharing is near and dear to my heart, then dare I say, *I could go on and on.* Of the *Whaikorero*, the oratory of the Maori, their speeches, narratives, songs, chants, they becoming one with body and soul. Guided by music, poetry, stories.

Often religious in nature, concept. Sacred, these, talents, gifts, the Maori gave in honor of their gods: the highest honor, themselves. By all means of expression available.

Modern technology allows me my own version of *Kapa haka*: group communication, chant. Uniting the culture of the Maori to an audience, with hand gestures, war dance foot stomping, intimidating foes. Witness the Maori *Kapa haka*, as performed by New Zealand's rugby players.

My gifts, enjoyed by a wide audience on poetry sites are found within the pages of my books of poetry. (Any foot stomping I do comes whenever I am too near a deadline.)

Any poetic semblance to the Maori, *Ta moko, tattoos*, of mine to theirs, comes, again, only, in the appreciation of art and my humble efforts at painting portraits. The Maori illustrated their artistic interpretations upon the canvas of the human body. Most proudly displayed.

Face carving/tattooing was mainly the sole right of men of rank, (and some women), revealing lineage. My rank, my name, credits me as an artist. And, author of three books.

Wings

When the windy breeze
Howls and moans, day and night
And the trees sway
And acorns drop

It is as if, in a movie
I see my past tap dancing
Across the tin roof top
Of my mountain home

And, just the very thought
Of those long ago days
Returns me to my teens
And back into a place and time

Where, never could I have envisioned
That the answer to the question
Of whether or not I could fly
Would come on the wings of poetry

The Succession

Disappointed, frustrated, I whined
Complained, Momma explaining
I had long had my turn
You are a big girl now

There is no need to cry. But, why
Oh, why must big girls not cry

And, why, oh why, did I not recall
As a baby, sitting in my papa's lap
It was as if I had lost my place
In line and never, ever

Would I find it
Or my babyhood again

At the tender age of four or five
I was told, the day I lost my place
In line, that I had once been Papa's
Baby girl, his darling little princess

But, alas. It was time
For baby brother to shine

Like a garden where blooms are enjoyed
For their fragrance, for their beauty
So too, I suppose I was their darling
In my baby hood's prime

Sadly, I yielded, unhappily
My coveted place in line

Tzemin Ition Tsai

Dr. Tzemin Ition Tsai (蔡澤民博士) was born in Tzemin Ition Tsai Taiwan, Republic of China, in 1957. He holds a Ph.D. in Chemical Engineering and two Masters of Science in Applied Mathematics and Chemical Engineering. He is an associate professor at the Asia University (Taiwan), editor of “Reading, Writing and Teaching” academic text. He also writes the long-term columns for Chinese Language Monthly in Taiwan.

He is a scholar with a wide range of expertise, while maintaining a common and positive interest in science, engineering and literature member.

He has won many national literary awards. His literary works have been anthologized and published in books, journals, and newspapers in more than 40 countries and have been translated into more than a dozen languages.

The Scenery of Small town

The grass is warm in the spring sunshine
Spread on the surrounding hillside boundlessly
Until the front endlessly and incomparably
The wind not only shakes the leaves of the old tree
Also slowly moving the clouds
Inviting that white like birds' feathers
Dyeing the clear sky

Colored flowers scattered everywhere
Give a subtle smell
The birds' quarrels are heard everywhere.
Like the sound of a bamboo flute resounding through in the air
It's all like telling
How beautiful is the scenery in this village?
Around the town
Bird's dance and floral fragrance
Wind unfolding hands
Trying to surround you in its embrace

Small temple at the end of the street
Unsealed fences and murals
Can't find any gemstones and brilliant bronze statues
And when you calm down
Sitting in front of the plate you can find
The sediment that belongs to your mind is actually mixed between the grass

The streetlight that just turned on is not so bright
The beggar sitting against all the wrinkles on face
Arms that are obviously thin and dry
Try to support his determined eyes
Look at your heart every day at the corner of the street

No longer eternal

this moment
When the sun is far from the stars
that moment
The drama that greets the moon is followed.

The beginning of the day at the end of the day
The sky usually won't
insomnia
Just forgot to count the promise that eternal

Twilight covered the sky
Black veil slowly spread
Countless stars
Full coverage of the sky
Cool night invasion
The song of birds and insects is coming to an end
Wake up silent bat
The frog and the cockroach opened the first ensemble
Belong to the night that is no longer eternal

This is a terrible transformation
When the light turns dark
Day also turned into night
Sparking eyes burning by alcohol
Extinguish glimpse of eternity
Quietly lying aside
Waiting to wake up again every other day

The egret's sigh: the old plow is really old

Pond-Water Road, which is in front of my face
Old plowing bull with a pair of blurred eyes
Who is exempting the plow on its neck?
Lamenting heart
If it's just the temporary mood of the old plowing bull
Not the sigh that no longer has to be enslaved
You surely clear in mind
I really shouldn't ask
Is this your heaven-born destiny?
When you also have the same gray-haired as I have?
More sadness will not help, we are not together until today
Come on
Let's sing together a song that celebrates the white head
Why don't you invite the old plow to rest?
Just for sit on a porch swing with but never need say a
word

Shareef Abdur Rasheed

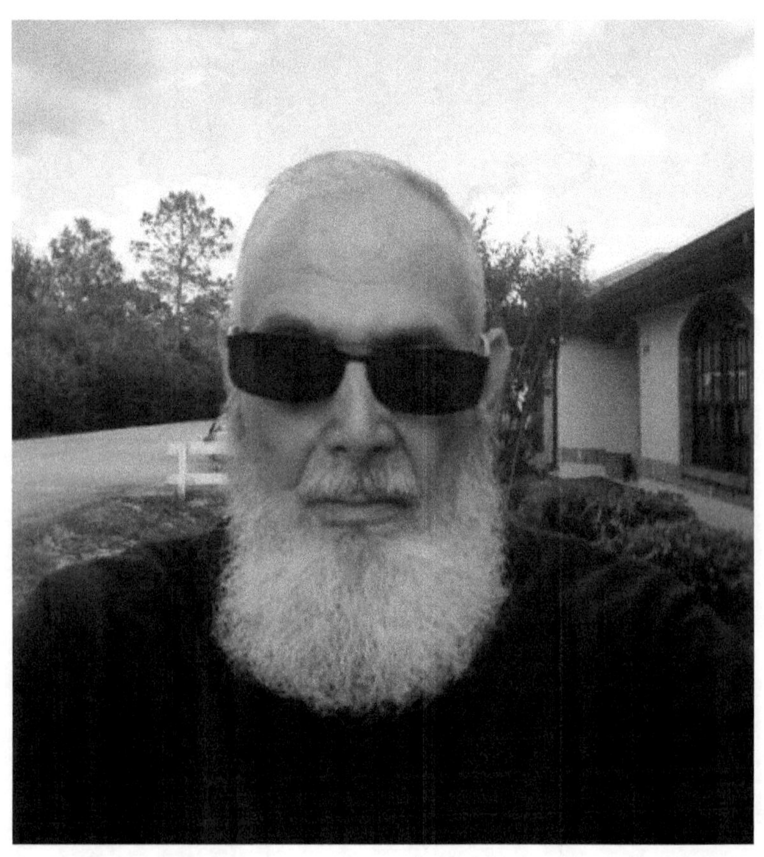

Shareef Abdur-Rasheed, AKA Zakir Flo was born and raised in Brooklyn, New York. His education includes Brooklyn College, Suffolk County Community College and Makkah, Saudi Arabia. He is a Veteran of the Viet Nam era, where in 1969 he reverted to his now reverently embraced Islamic Faith. He is very active in the Islamic community and beyond with his teachings, activism and his humanity.

Shareef's spiritual expression comes through the persona of "Zakir Flo" . Zakir is Arabic for "To remind". Never silent, Shareef Abdur-Rasheed is always dropping science, love, consciousness and signs of the time in rhyme.

Shareef is the Patriarch of the Abdur-Rasheed Family with 9 Children (6 Sons and 3 Daughters) and 41 Grandchildren (24 Boys and 17 Girls).

For more information about Shareef, visit his personal FaceBook Page at :

https://www.facebook.com/shareef.abdurrasheed1
https://zakirflo.wordpress.com

triangle

going way back
thousands of years
southeast Asia the place
Polynesian peoples traced
migrated to other places
in time became Polynesian
triangle where Maori peoples
reside
Maori peoples blessed
scored high in intellect
especially in respect to
navigation, astronomy, artful
ability
carving, weaving their specialty
as were long sea journeys like
the one to Aotearoa
Known today as New Zealand
New Zealand where they settled
coming from triangle of islands
Hawai'i, Easter to Aotearoa,
New Zealand
the indigenous people cut from
the earth in harmony with love,
in love with harmony
respecting the bounties on
land and sea
gave praise continuously
gratitude framed attitude of
responsibility to treat mother
earth's treasures seriously,
respectfully
as indigenous be generally
caretakers of the abode of
humanity

the me

feeding all fleshly sensations
yourself being the only relation
wrapped up in yourself
to you there is no one else
every word you say begins
and ends with me
beyond that you can't see
narcissistic obsession
dictates your direction
defines who you be
the selfish manifestation of
me, me, me
this is todays sad commentary
there is traces of it in everybody
but we must fight to do what's
right, and care and be aware of
somebody else besides yourself
put selfishness on the shelf
replacing me with we
exhibit mercy for the forlorn
wretched, miserable without hope
for they had no control to whom
and where they were born
into stark poverty ignored, scorned
compassion for them who see no
light at tunnel's end,
tunnel just goes on 'n ' on
as lives end never to see an end
put yourself there my friend
it could have been you
but for the grace of god
there i go

but you were spared
so that perhaps you can care
for those in despair
givers cup always run over
drinking from overflow
cup stays full
not so the taker
greedy fool
who chose to take from those
who needed to be given
await a telling fate after their
death replace their living
for in the end it's all weighed
on the scale
to determine if
one’s short stay on earth
succeeded or failed

Dem.,

trifling, making something
out of nothing
ignoring things important
dem doing what dem ought
not
true dem not Johnny
on spot
caring for the have nots
dem who don't have a pot
to piss
never mind window to throw it
when you living on sidewalks
no one wants to know it
walk pass you right there
what the hell they care
this is Amerikkka my dear
capitalism, thee schism of is'ms
don't see them
dem exist not
dem don't got none what make
machine run ===$$$$$==>
richest nation on dear mother earth
can care less for homeless
that often their system set the table
that rendered them disabled
to put roof over head, food on table
while wall st. play for high stakes
as for poverty stricken dem taking
not giving
dem exist not who have no chips
in the pot
says dem greedy none stop

"So the F what..,
all we give a $#!+ about is what
we got "
say it again..,
"So the F what..,"
all we give a $#!+ about is what
we got "
f dem have nots
another day in the land of the free
home of the brave
the one they killed for and took
and kidnapped millions of human beings
to work and cultivate for free
dem not free dem slaves
to the devil who got them chained
to their flesh craves
but won't go well for them in the
grave
god won't bless the land of
' just-me '
this is not the land you call liberty
until justice rings true, fulfilled
justice is what makes one free
Ceee ???

Kimberly Burnham

See yourself in the pattern. As a 28-year-old photographer, Kimberly Burnham appreciated beauty. Then an ophthalmologist diagnosed her with a genetic eye condition saying, "Consider life, if you become blind." She discovered a healing path with insight, magnificence, and vision. Today, a poet and neurosciences expert with a PhD in Integrative Medicine, Kimberly's life mission is to change the global face of brain health. Using health coaching, Reiki, Matrix Energetics, craniosacral therapy, acupressure, and energy medicine, she supports people in their healing from nervous system and chronic pain issues. A current project is taking pages from medical literature and turning them into visual poetry by circling the words of the poem and coloring in the rest—recycling words into color and drawing out the poem.

http://www.NerveWhisperer.Solutions
https://www.linkedin.com/in/kimberlyburnham

Richly Textured Peace

"Whakaturi" a richly textured Maori word
one meaning is obstinate
to be unyielding or stubborn
turn a deaf ear
or pay no attention

Giving the impression of a spoiled child
or arrogant man
a busy woman too harried to listen

A second meaning is to mollify
make peace with
or appease
as if we can make peace without paying attention
or perhaps find peace by clinging stubbornly to life

The third meaning wrapped into this word
"whakaturi" is a love token or a keepsake
something we hold to unyieldingly
or would give anything
to hold onto the love and peace it represents

"Whakaturi" we have a choice
how we see the world
through the eyes of a stubborn child
peacemaker
or a giver of gifts

Finding Self Surrounded In Peace

In Niuean spoken on Niue Island
the Rock of Polynesia
coral land in the midst of the South Pacific
"Loto" means inside
within
between

"Lotoloto" amongst or in the middle of
in the heart of desire
is "fakalotomafola"
"mafola" peace
to be at peace in one's heart or mind

"Fakalotomafola" also to appease
"to fakalotoma fola e au a ia ke he mena fakaalofa"
"I will appease him with a present"
or give myself the gift of peace

"Kia fakalotomafola a koe"
to be at peace with yourself
as if to give yourself a peace gift
surrounding yourself with peace
finding yourself within

#2 New Zealand Just Behind Iceland in Peace

10 years
New Zealand never slipping below
4th almost perfect marks
Global Peace Index
top marks in health status
above average education jobs and earnings
yet the gap between rich and poor
distressing 20% of New Zealand's 4.7 million citizens

Peace "rangimārie" in Maori
some people say starts with a smile
but ask anyone who lives
in peaceful countries
it is the other way around

Peaceful nations enjoy
lower interest rates
stronger currency
higher foreign investment
better political stability
greater perceived happiness

The economic impact of violence
quantifiable $14.76 trillion in 2017
12.4% of total global gross domestic product
about $1,988 per person on this spinning planet
almost 20 percent of the average world citizen's yearly income

Says the Institute for Economics and Peace
of 163 independent states and territories
99.7% of the world's population
23 indicators
societal safety and security
a peek at ongoing domestic and international conflicts
degree of militarization

Global peace is declining
making the world less peaceful
compared to any time in the last decade
refugee numbers skyrocketing
1% of the world population
highest level in modern history
and the United States drops seven spots to 121st
well behind Iceland (1) where peace is call "friður"
New Zealand (2)
Cuba (81) and China (114)
a little too close to the least peaceful country in the world
Syria (163) seriously lacking in "salām"

Elizabeth E. Castillo

Elizabeth Esguerra Castillo

Elizabeth Esguerra Castillo is a multi-awarded and an Internationally-Published Contemporary Author/Poet and a Professional Writer / Creative Writer / Feature Writer / Journalist / Travel Writer from the Philippines. She has 2 published books, "Seasons of Emotions" (UK) and "Inner Reflections of the Muse", (USA). Elizabeth is also a co-author to more than 60 international anthologies in the USA, Canada, UK, Romania, India. She is a Contributing Editor of Inner Child Magazine, USA and an Advisory Board Member of Reflection Magazine, an international literary magazine. She is a member of the American Authors Association (AAA) and PEN International.

Web links:

Facebook Fan Page

https://free.facebook.com/ElizabethEsguerraCastillo

Google Plus

https://plus.google.com/u/0/+ElizabethCastillo

Let's Do the Haka

Tengata Whenua-

The mythical Polynesian island

Let's visit the marae-

Dance the haka all day.

Enjoy the hangi feast

With food cooked in earthly ovens

Let's do the haka dance

Sweep the night away.

Beauty in Diversity

I dreamed of a world where there is no disparity

One, where there is unity among nations

Though of different beliefs, or of varied skin colors

There would be equality among all races.

You may be white, I may be brown, and he may be yellow

Outer appearance may seem to make us different from each other

But this doesn't mean that racial discrimination we must allow

For we shall traverse the same destination one fine day.

Ancient Arabia

Hegra, built by the Nabeteans of Petra Jordan-
In the 1st Century, B.C, resting place for caravans and defense
Mada-in Saleh in Saudi Arabia
Half as old as time.

The magical pitch dark crept through the night-
And I saw the vivid ancient carvings on the wall
Once one visits this ancient ruins of Dedan,
Grotesque images flow on your mind, of antlers and beasts lurking.

The narrow valley amidst bare red sandstones will stun you
To the west lies the Red Sea and the east is the ancient gold mine of Midian
Dedan mentioned in the Old Testament tells of the descendants of Abraham
From his wife Ketura and the Tablet of the People.

Mineans traded with the Egyptians
Sphinx-like monsters guard the tombstones
And in an inscription on a sarcophagus in the Ptolemaic Period
An Egyptian priest was depicted who happens to be a Minean.

Nizar Sartawi

Nizar Sartawi is a poet, translator, essayist, and columnist. He was born in Sarta, Palestine, in 1951. He is a member of literary and cultural organizations, including the Jordanian Writers Association (Jordan), General Union of Arab Writers (Cairo), Poetry Posse (U.S.), Inner Child Press International (U.S.), Bodgani (Belgium), and Axlepin Publishing (the Philippines). He has participated in poetry readings and international forums and festivals in numerous countries, including Jordan, Lebanon, Kosovo, Palestine, Morocco, Egypt, and India. Sartawi's poems have been translated into several languages. His poetry has been anthologized and published in many anthologies, journals, and newspapers in Arab countries, the U.S., Australia, Indonesia, Bosnia, Italy, India, the Philippines, and Taiwan.

Sartawi has published more than 20 books of poetry and poetry translation. His last poetry collection, *My Shadow,* was published in June, 2017 by Inner Child Press in the U.S.

For the last seven years, Sartawi has been working on poetry translation from English to Arabic and Arabic to English. This includes his Arabic poetry translation project, "Arab Contemporary Poets Series" in which 13 bilingual books have been published so far. He also has translated poems for a number of contemporary international poets such as, Veronica Golos, Elaine Equi; William S. Peters; Kalpna Singh-Chitnis; Nathalie Handal, Naomi Shihab Nye; Candice James; Ashok Bhargava; Santiago Villafania, Virginia Jasmin Pasalo; Rosa Jamali; Taro Aizu; Fahredin Shehu, and many others.

Tattoo

When his turn came
he stepped forward
and kneeled
his eyes wide open
gazing at the maori face

Rawiri,
please… a nice tattoo!

What kind of *moko*?
Where do you want to wear it?

His right hand quivered
frantically flew up
and cupped his left breast
I want a heart
here, he said,
a heart above my heart

a *manawa!*
mattered the tattoo guru

~ ~ ~ ~

Since then
he's been obsessed
with his *manawa*
the second heart
chiseled
upon his breast.

For there
– behind each shape

each curve
each circle
line
and dot –
his life
his journey
days on earth
the faces that he loved
were all
inscribed

a rendezvous on the plage de versoix

around 10:45 she arrived
her little poodle
proudly prancing ahead of her
she climbed down the iron stairs
moved close to the waters of Lake Geneva
unfolded her striped mat
spread it on the silver pebbles
sat down
and waited

11 sharp
quack quack quack
a choir of four ducks
out of the lake
marching in a queue
her fluffy poodle jumped
on his hind legs
laughing and dancing
and she was up on her feet too

bonjour
yap yap
quack quack

and all six went for the usual walk
on the Plage de Vesoix

haiku

they all stopped weeping

when the gentle west wind blew

the weeping willows

hülya
n.
yılmaz

Born in Turkey, hülya n. yılmaz presently serves as full-time faculty at Penn State and as the Director of Editing Services at Inner Child Press. Her academic publications dwell on literary relations between the West and the Islamic East and on gender conceptualizations within the context of Islam. Dr. yılmaz had her formal initiation as a creative writer in the U.S. Her published works include *Trance* –a tri-lingual book of poetry, *Aflame* –memoirs in verse and *An Aegean Breeze of Peace* –a poem collection she has co-authored with Demetrius Trifiatis. Poetry by hülya appeared in excess of fifty international anthologies.

hülya n. yılmaz, Ph.D.

Links

Personal Web Site
https://hulyasfreelancing.com

Personal Blog Site
https://dolunaylaben.wordpress.com/

The Maori

members of New Zealand's Polynesian population
with their unique history of instrumental musicality
succumbed to the insatiable European taste for acculturation
under Abel Tasman's schools of indoctrination
and were forced to lose their voices' authenticity

they belonged to the 14th century Hawaikian migration

while some of their chants and dance steps are said to be still alive
their poetry's audible and visual soul-filled domination
which had unequivocally been enchanting before
were quite suddenly not there anymore

the year was 1642 – an era of turmoil
nothing less nothing more

The King Movement their courageous and heroic initiative
was conceived to put an end to the occupiers' selling of their land
but the occupying government of the colonial White
insisted on its free land-for all-chanting left and right
thus arrived at everyone's doorstep in 1859 all upright
the first of the worst The First Taranaki War

successful sieges by British troops and militia
and equally successful Maorian victories ensued
then came the Second Taranaki War and the Waikato War
eventually unfolding the region's final kill-all conflict

coined by the Europeans as "the fire in the fern"
it also had for the Maori reached a point of no return
as *te riri pakeha* – "the white man's anger" they branded
that assault
knowing now too well to take these matters more seriously
than afore

what happened then is nothing new you see
The King Movement and its aftermath ceased to be
hence goes the story of a people named The Maori

the babies' Blues

we grew up amid the chants
and the dance of our elderly

before we learned how to walk
we had already acquired the talk
of The White that pierced our land
and then sold it piece by piece by hand

our parents were charged with a dire task
to embark on many a wars for us was their call

we needed protection from *te riri pakeha*
at first we thought it came from mayhaw
it was however nothing at which we could gnaw
"the white man's anger" grew like mountains with snow

our elderlies speak no more so we no longer know
if we will ever have a safe shelter a safe place to go

1987

was a memorable year my child
a glorious time in our lives
when we chanted above and beyond
in our very own genuine Maori tongue

our *hongi* was no longer outlawed as taboo
nor was our *haangi* seen as a place to voodoo

our long-ago-ancestors had a different destiny
their own land was under The White custody
as was everything else that once was of The Maori
so there were many a wars to defend our dignity

you now belong to a generation that will steadily prosper
don't ever yield your home to anything that claims to be a
foster

Teresa E. Gallion

Teresa E. Gallion was born in Shreveport, Louisiana and moved to Illinois at the age of 15. She completed her undergraduate training at the University of Illinois Chicago and received her master's degree in Psychology from Bowling Green State University in Ohio. She retired from New Mexico state government in 2012.

She moved to New Mexico in 1987. While writing sporadically for many years, in 1998 she started reading her work in the local Albuquerque poetry community. She has been a featured reader at local coffee houses, bookstores, art galleries, museums, libraries, Outpost Performance Space, the Route 66 Festival in 2001 and the State of Oklahoma's Poetry Festival in Cheyenne, Oklahoma in 2004. She occasionally hosts an open mic.

Teresa's work is published in numerous Journals and anthologies. She has two CDs: *On the Wings of the Wind* and *Poems from Chasing Light*. She has published three books: *Walking Sacred Ground, Contemplation in the High Desert* and *Chasing Light.*

Chasing Light was a finalist in the 2013 New Mexico/Arizona Book Awards.

The surreal high desert landscape and her personal spiritual journey influence the writing of this Albuquerque poet. When she is not writing, she is committed to hiking the enchanted landscapes of New Mexico. You may preview her work at

http://bit.ly/1aIVPNq or http://bit.ly/13IMLGh

Maori Culture

You imprinted the landscape centuries
before the Europeans arrived.
Since the 1960s, you have been in a cultural
revival and activists for social justice.

Like other indigenous people,
you hold your identity,
fight for pieces of the land you lost
struggle with economic development
and a place in the political landscape.

Your rich culture with songs, art,
dance, and deep spiritual beliefs
sustained you through the centuries
as you made New Zealand home.

Glorious Memories

Rain slaps my window today.
Gray New Mexico skies
are an occasional treat.

My muse gets cozy
in my favorite chair
and wants to play.
I open my arms.

It is raining just hard enough
to feel like a gentle massage.
I feel the delight
of memories pulled from my bank.
No one sees the glow on my cheeks.

Do I want to share this moment?
I'd rather watch the rain
wipe my windows clean
and cleanse my spirit.

Last night I dreamed about
Mount St. Michel, Machu Piccu,
Godafoss Waterfall, Sahara Desert,
the Matterhorn. The imagery
followed me into the morning rain.

I take leave here to embrace
joy and wonder. Perhaps I will see you
on the other side of bliss dancing
in your own glorious memories.

Word Offering

It is the end of Fall.
My seeds lay down to sleep
and the color fest is done.

Everything prepares for
deep slumber nestled
in winter's white blanket.

The dream weaver prepares
to plant stories
in the hearts of heavy sleepers.

I am ready to rest
and watch my word colony
cultivate its spring offering.

Ashok
K.
Bhargava

Ashok Bhargava is a poet, writer, community activist, public speaker, management consultant and a keen photographer. Based in Vancouver, he has published several collections of his poems: Riding the Tide, Mirror of Dreams, A Kernel of Truth, Skipping Stones, Half Open Door and Lost in the Morning Calm. His poetry has been published in various literary magazines and anthologies.

Ashok is a Poet Laureate and poet ambassador to Japan, Korea and India. He is founder of WIN: Writers International Network Canada. Its main objective is to inspire, encourage, promote and recognize writers of diverse genres, artists and community leaders. He has received many accolades including Nehru Humanitarian Award for his leadership of Writers International Network Canada, Poets without Borders Peace Award for his journeys across the globe to celebrate peace and to create alliances with poets, and Kalidasa Award for creative writings.

Mists of Time

I know
what I do not know about
the wonder that lies
behind mythical chants and dances.

Is it to
reach the beginning of eternity
with tender whispers and
rhythmic stamping of the feet?

Is it to celebrate
the ocean-waves
that advance, recede, shimmer
and break like tears?

I know over your isolated shores
echoing songs are like
reading words with mouth and
writing history with dancing feet.

Maori you have created
your own universe
your own self
in the endless mists of time.

Fragile Stones

I love stones
revere them
admire them
talk to them.
My poems arise out of stones
in the morning silence
strong and
poignant.
I worship stones
bathe them
cloth them
deities reside in them
Behind the stone temple door
I utter prayers
to invoke them
to receive stone blessings.
Stones are my friends
they shift and lean over
to speak to me
in perfect stillness.
In my dreams
they open up
bloom like flowers
sweet and fragrant.

Can't You Feel The Spirits Moving?

Why do you look at me
as if you were the moon
distant
smiling over the ocean
as impatient waves break
in your amber light?
Why do you look at me
as if you were the sun
sovereign
laughing on a zealous day
that burns the dust
and boils my thirsty blood?
Why do you look at me
as if
the earth loves you
the planets pursue you
the angels have blessed you
with solitude?
Why do you look at me
in the cold air that blows
over the morning's damp skin
as she wraps herself in her solar poncho?

If from the blue Sky you look down again
be careful how you look at me.

The Return

Our plans to drive through
the wind-swept valley
giant boulders
crumbling rocks
prickly pears and
Joshua trees
did not include
you at the doorway of a sushi place
in a red blouse
with a tempura smile
sake-warm hands
waiting to come out
from hiding.
You must have
wished for such a moment
otherwise how
would that be possible.

Caroline 'Ceri Naz' Nazareno

Caroline Nazareno-Gabis a.k.a. Ceri Naz, born in Anda, Pangasinan known as a 'poet of peace and friendship', is a multi-awarded poet, journalist, editor, publicist, linguist, educator, and women's advocate.

Graduated cum laude with the degree of Bachelor of Elementary Education, specialized in General Science at Pangasinan State University. Ceri have been a voracious researcher in various arts, science and literature. She volunteered in Richmond Multicultural Concerns Society, TELUS World Science, Vancouver Art Gallery, and Vancouver Aquarium.

She was privileged to be chosen as one of the Directors of Writers Capital International Foundation (WCIF), Member of the Poetry Posse, one of the Board of Directors of Galaktika ATUNIS Magazine based in Albania; the World Poetry Canada and International Director to Philippines; Global Citizen's Initiatives Member, Association for Women's rights in Development (AWID) and Anacbanua. She has been a 4th Placer in World Union of Poets Poetry Prize 2016, Writers International Network-Canada ''Amazing Poet 2015'', The Frang Bardhi Literary Prize 2014 (Albania), the sair-gazeteci or Poet-Journalist Award 2014 (Tuzla, Istanbul, Turkey) and World Poetry Empowered Poet 2013 (Vancouver, Canada).

Hongi

Breath to breath
A shield, a canopy
Maori's verdant garden
Like paintings of smiles
keeping silver moons,
Strokes of kiwi
Stamped with freedom.

Echoes of life,
Interfacing desires
From North's face,
From South's tongue,
From East's forehead,
From West's lips,
From all life's direction,
Of body and spirit,
Reshaping hopes.

Flowers and Rainbow

It was early morning
when I heard a different sound
from the neighbourhood,
blended in hostility and vexation,

It was like a fall of
the red hibiscus,
vincas and plumbago
that I once knew,
the source of strength and happiness,
I've missed the dragonflies wandering
I used to catch
even in the afternoon,
waiting for the reassuring crepuscular rays,
though sometimes, life is so unkind.
I could still see the redolence
of a blooming rainbow
in love.

Sculptures of Time

I am an unwritten poem.
Inked in the farmer's land,
Soulfully sketched in the chambers
Of distance,
Of illusions
From the midnight oils
Burning,
Constant change.

I am the Waiata
The carvings and knots
Between miracle and mystery,
Between spring and autumn,
Between lands and oceans,
Between the earth and sky,
Of my ancestor's breath

Swapna Behera

Swapna Behera is a bilingual contemporary poet, author, translator and editor from Odisha, India .She was a teacher from 1984 to 2015 . Her stories, poems and articles are widely published in National and International journals, and ezines, and are translated into different national and International languages. She has penned four books. She was conferred upon the Prestigious International Poesis Award of Honor at the 2nd Bharat Award for Literature as Jury in 2015, The Enchanting Muse Award in India World Poetree Festival 2017, World Icon of Peace Award in 2017, and the Pentasi B World Fellow Poet in 2017.. She is the recipient of Gold Cross Of Wisdom Award ,the medal for The Best Teachers of the World from World Union of Poets in 2018,and The LIfe time Achievement Award ,The Best Planner Award and The Sahitya Shiromani Award from the Literati Cosmos Society 2018 .She is the Ambassador of Humanity by Hafrikan Prince Art World Africa 2018 and an official member of World Nation's Writers Union ,Kazakhstan2018. At present she is the manager at Large, Planner and Columnist of The Literati,the administrator of several poetic groups ,the member of the Special Council of Five of World Union of Poets and the Cultural Ambassador of Inner Child Press U.S.

Transforming a Window

In the Maori village
Sovereign hunting of love
Pulsating odour of Hangi
Vibrates the wind
In transit of a new portrait
The disciplined endorsement
The gushing streams near the Marae
Collaborative jingles
Lush green pastures
Infinite earth catering a collective life
Where every I merges with WE
The flora and fauna,
the green ravines
food on charcoal
rejuvenating symphony
Where the protocol of community life exists
The leader stimulates the group
Each one greets with Hongi
Emancipating the vivacity
grandeur of solidarity
yes ,the window is transformed
into a door to sky ......

[N.B- Marae is the meeting ground
Hongi is greeting by pressing the nose and forehead
Hangi is food cooked in underground smelting]

That Morning......

That morning the Sun rose in the sky
My verses reflected the rays
My pen was ready to bleed
My paper spread its chest to take the bullets or ballots

That morning my fingers were playing
Marbles to decode the passions
The anecdotes of past with a fusion to present
I had an action plan ready
My alphabets were data based

That morning I feel detoxifying my cells
My anger ,my pain, my insult, my sorrow volatilised
My eyes desperate to see the green crop field
The melody of the tribal women
The kids opening the yellow cells of the jackfruit
My thirst was quenched

That morning I was pregnant with an eternal wave
I smiled; gleamed with joy
Perhaps I became the queen
Of the Universe
Picking my pen
I sat on the pertinent throne

I was tenacious to be the radical rhythm
Of a dynamic rhyme
Not with the synthetic juice or robotic salads
But with the fresh water of the oasis
Not with drooping eyes
but with my pen to culminate

I sat in between
The kids with dyslexia or visually challenged
Girls with Rett syndrome;
The rape victims; child or women
I was rotating in my axiom
Yes that morning I was audacious
To scribble a melody for them
The Anthem of victory.....

As A Dot

Me !!! Me !!!
A timid versatility
On the sea shore
Or
The prelude
of the horizon
Have the trust
Strong enough
To see your scribble
On the palms of
the trembling shadow
A string of a violin
A grass blade
smilies of dew drops
Where all emotions merge
To one emptiness
As a dot I swim
As a dot I swim - - - -

William S. Peters Sr.

Bill's writing career spans a period of over 50 years. Being first Published in 1972, Bill has since went on to Author in excess of 40 additional Volumes of Poetry, Short Stories, etc., expressing his thoughts on matters of the Heart, Spirit, Consciousness and Humanity. His primary focus is that of Love, Peace and Understanding!

Bill says . . .

I have always likened Life to that of a Garden. So, for me, Life is simply about the Seeds we Sow and Nourish. All things we "Think and Do", will "Be" Cause and eventually manifest itself to being an "Effect" within our own personal "Existences" and "Experiences" . . . whether it be Fruit, Flowers, Weeds or Barren Landscapes! Bill highly regards the Fruits of his Labor and wishes that everyone would thus go on to plant "Lovely" Seeds on "Good Ground" in their own Gardens of Life!

to connect with Bill, he is all things Inner Child

www.iaminnerchild.com

Personal Web Site

www.iamjustbill.com

Maori

We know of the oceans
And how they speak
A language
Calling for us
To venture its waves
And currents

We look to horizons
And the distant lands
Waiting to be discovered

We know of the civil tones
That gives cause
For the embrace
Of man
And his humanity

We know of love,
That of our people
And those we have yet
To meet

We have an identity
That belongs to
Us alone

We mark our flesh
With our pride
And ink
As we dance
Worshipping the Gods
Of Creation

We are Maori

A tribute to love

There is a spirit that prevails
That carries my warmth
And all that I deem worthwhile
Within her breast

She is my smiles,
My laughter,
My tears
And my
Happily ever after

She is the wind
That makes my wings
Feel integral,
The soft breeze
That carries the fragrance
Of the blossoming
Of my dreams
Of the future
And that of my
Now-ness

She gives me purpose!

My prowess
Is enhanced
By her presence
And I dance
Because of her
Essence

Her embrace,
The light upon her face
That leaks from her eyes
Staves off

Any demise
That dare approach me
For she alone
Is my reproach
For the shade or shadows
Made in the meadows
That lie
At the feet
Of the mountains
I have come to climb

I think my self
To be a poet,
But she is my rhyme
And my ability
To envision
And conjure
The things of
Magnificence
. . . .
Does that make any sense ? . . .

Well it doesn't have to,
For I have her... love
And in these lines
I hope you too can find
A reason
To . . .
Pay your own
Tribute
To Love

The Anatomy of a poem

Disclaimer : this is not a Sonnet

What is a poem ?

Many would say that it is
About the rhyme scheme . .
You know such things as
Shoe
And do
And you
On cue
And what you know,
And what you once knew

Others would say
It is about
Your iambic pentameter
You know,
The footsteps of the beat
And your syllabic execution
The feet man, the feet

Many would say
Does the poem
Move me,
Take me away,
Allow me to play
In the poet's visions
And dreams
Their hopes
Their fears . .
Will I laugh, smile
Or shed some tears

Some look for messages,
And many of us poets
Have none
Worthwhile sharing . . .
What happened to the poet's . . .
And the readers . . .
Caring ?

Was the poem
A throw-away
Or stow-away
To read some other time,
One which we never quite seem
To get around to

Was the offered poem
Endearing . . .
Did you find a line
Or verse
That gave cause
For your swearing
Tearing
Or fearing
Today,
Tomorrow
And what may come
Or did the poem leave you hanging
Looking for that
Sum-mation
About its position,
Stance
Or station

Was the poem
Informative
Or just another
*expletive

You depleted
When you almost
Completed
Reading
The humble words
Of we
The struggling poets
Who search for words
To touch you
In a place of understanding . . .

After all,
We poets
Like so many others
Mainly just wish to be . .
Heard

There are many aspects and
Endless possibilities
To what a poem may be,
And quite frankly
There is not enough paper
In the entire world
To describe
Its poet-ential,

So I will leave you with this . . .
My simple anatomy is
That a poem should kiss you
In a place
That the Sun
Does not shine . . .
No, not in the accepted respect,
But it should help you
To uncover
And detect
A piece of

Your missing self
That you have put
On that now
Dusty shelf
Of
Spirit,
Consciousness,
Compassion,
Humanity . . .

It should help you see clearly
The insanity
We endure
While taking you pleasantly
Or tersely away
To explore
The possibilities
Of the beauty abound
Within you
Or without

From the darkness comes the light,
Our courage is spawned
In the womb of our fright
And wrongs are reconciled
By the 'right'
And each day
Is birthed from
A night

May this humble anatomy
Serve my own plight
In seeking to write
something meaningful

Poetic offerings
My verse is FREE !

December

2018

Features

~ * ~

Rose Terranova Cirigliano

Joanna Kalinowska

Emir Sokolovic

Ashokchakravarthy Tholana

I
Fly
because
I Can
...said the Dreamer to the world.
www.iamjustbill.com

Rose
Terranova
Cirigliano

I am a retired teacher; 17 years in the classroom, (Junior High), and then 8 years on TV. I wrote, hosted, and produced educational programs for the Catholic Diocese of Brooklyn and Queens. On the side I was the director of a parish theater group mounting two productions each year, one a musical play, and the other a Cabaret. I am a classically trained singer, and did recitals from 1983 through 2000. I met Lewis Crystal in 1979 when I worked at HBJ Bookstore with him and Brigitte. I've always written poetry, from when I was in my teens. Lewis enabled me to make some of my private writing public. And I have been grateful ever since. I currently edit a seasonal anthology for and online group FM, and other works from an international group of authors through a small publishing company, ROSE BOOKS, an affiliate of AVENUE U PUBLISHERS, [Lewis Crystal (owner)].

Look back to look ahead

Excavation underway…
dining room corner…
unearthing a 1924 Crosley record player and radio
belonged to my aunt, a gift from her father on her 17th birthday.

The debris of at least 20 years…
when it was placed in that corner….
after her death….
the last major transition point in my life….
On the way to the next…

photographs and memories….
jewelry that has been missing for years…
hahaha... lots of old paperwork…
finally tossed….

what to keep, what to sell, what to give away or toss…
lots of dust irritating my nose and throat…
and my hands...itchy….

Found an old letter that I never sent…
the preamble to an attempt to process my life that was….unfinished...
I was high and hopeful….for 8 months….
Then reflective….

At my peak….

been a slow descent….

Time for a change…
time for casting off the debris of this life
that will ultimately land in a dumpster….
So I'll toss it myself….
Don't want to leave a mess in my wake…

My life has been a mess and a jumble
and an honest attempt to find happiness
and stay away from pain….
I did not succeed….

But I hope I leave something of worth behind
to justify it all.

In a World Gone Mad

"Money makes the world go around the world
go around the world go around, t
hat clinking clanking sound,
it makes the world go round..." [Cabaret].

People want power,
control,
ease,
toys, amusements,
things...many things,
sound systems, electronics, computers,
lavish homes, cars, yachts, planes,
etc etc etc….

But they need people to take care of all these things,
for them;
they are too lazy to care for everything themselves.
But they have to pay them to do it.
Wouldn't slaves be better?

Well, you still have to clothe and feed them,
and supply them with some kind of housing….
So….hmmm…
what about letting them have the illusion of
control and some power,
little bits and pieces of what we have,
(after all, we know from history that if we
make things uncomfortable for them
they might just revolt...lol),

and in exchange,
they give us everything we want?
Sounds good to me… so, how we gonna do that?

Hmmmm…. Well, it won't be easy to fool them….
Or maybe it would be….
PT Barnum did say, "There's a sucker born every minute!"
Or did he?
Who cares… Let the games begin…

What we end up with are two classes….
The very rich and powerful, and the minions.

Of course there is always going to be the idiot fringe,
the weak, the crippled, the stupid,
the defeated, the depressed, the mentally ill….

They make great scapegoats for our plan….
After all we need someone to blame when things go wrong.
…

…. Are we there yet???

Fact or Fakery

We sign virtual petitions
Expressing our rage
We go on marches wearing hats
Or in support of our children
And nothing changes

We read that we are hacked
And manipulated by pros
We question what is FAKE and what is FACT
And nothing changes

We post memes in support of our position
Engage in arguments with total strangers
Arguing in poli-meme-speak
And nothing changes

We are stuck hoping for November
Hoping there will be a miraculous turnout
That will somehow miraculously
Stem the course of disaster
And ???? what if nothing changes?

Joanna
Kalinowska

Joanna Kalinowska

Joanna Kalinowska, says about herself, that she was born under a wandering star. She, as a child (a daughter of an officer), often moved from one place to another. These constant changes taught her the openness and the willingness to meet new people and places.

She spent many years in Poland. Fifteen years ago she moved to Italy.

She has always been writing but she publishes now. Her book "Ascoltando Azzurro –Wsłuchana w błękit" was written so that people who speak different languages can express the same feelings. Three volumes of her poetry were edited and her poems were printed in various anthologies and magazines.

She writes and publishes in two languages, both Polish and Italian. She loves these two countries. They are her homelands.
She arranged "The Amici Italia-Polonia Association". Its headquarters there is in Taranto — the city where she lives and works.

She is a teacher, but she actually works as a translator and an activist of the Polish community.

She is a member of the Warsaw Association of Literature's Translators. Joanna works for the Italian literary-cultural group "La Vallisa", too. She also cooperates with magazine of this group.

She is the initiator and organizer of many cultural and social events.

Carrier of mystery

carrier of mystery
smiles to herself
she sees the universe enclosed in a droplet
she is a priestess
guarding the gates between the worlds
and she is the gate herself
chosen by a soul
what's going to come back to her?
it is in her but it is not her
it feeds on her blood
but it gives her pure light
from which love will flow
the purest in the world

Living ...

I live with what is left of the spirit of my childhood
I wake up and see the sun again
the morning greets me
allowing for new discoveries during the trip
I have grown little bit
but I am always this cloud of dreams
I move forward because the world is spinning
and if I remain motionless
I will be on the dark side of the moon
where a man cannot see anything
I go because I do not want to be late
for to go forward means to read and write
study life and understand the world
I go to meet the upcoming dreams
and when I wander enough
to be able to stop I will turn around and see
that I am that girl
I explored the meaning of cognition
explored the things that faced me
and that's why I know those who are like me, like us,
have wings
that lift them above the clouds of reality
rising into this area of heaven
where all dreams are beautiful
and it is possible to touch them

Wall

the wall is just ... just ...
facing you and it has a closed window
on the right there is photo of your mother as a young girl
with a look and smile of a startled doe
which resembles our daughter's smile so much

on the windowsill there are flowers and a statuette of elf
bought in Ireland
it was our honeymoon and you woke me up with kisses
it seemed that we were beginning a journey of life holding
hands

it's clear that the wall is there, it exists like me
sometimes you will stop with a blind sight
but I have a heart that has never stopped to loving you

do not pretend that nothing has happened,
do not ignore me in this way
kill this silence before it finishes us
it is a silence that has a magnetically destructive power
and a beam of radiation suppressing every sound

get angry ... raise your voice…cry ... cry
I am here, in front of you,
How can you not hear me?
Look into my eyes, you do not see me,
honey, you do not see me anymore?
show passion ... anger ... jealousy ...
any reaction but show it to me
I'm screaming and you're silent
with unseeing eyes and closed mouth

silence...
outside the window, the rain stuns the grass
heads of flowers rise ... and only one tear

I close my eyes ... silence ... I disappear ...
only the white wall remains

Translation- Alicja Maria Kuberska
Language consultation- Maureen Clifford

Emir Sokolovic

Sokolović Emir was born in 1961. His works have been translated into Italian, Polish, English, French... He has been published in many anthologies and collections. He is the creator and director of the prestigious international literary festival "Pero Živodraga Živković". So far he published:

- „Dove e perche/ Gdje i zašto“ – Edizione Foreman, Bergamo 1983.
- „Apokalipsa“ – intermedijalni projekat TV Zetel, 1994.
- „Una era canna allora/ Bio je tada trska“ – autorsko izdanje 1998.
- „Paris – ili zalud je razapinjeti Krista“ – autorsko izdanje 1999.
- „Oslobađanje“ – autorsko izdanje 2003.
- „Lako je jurišati na nebo koje ćuti...“ – autorsko izdanje 2011.
- „Una era canna allora“ – Casa Editrice „Rocco Carabba“ 2013.
- „Poetica demonica“ – „Kultura snova“ 2014.
- „Ples među podsjenama“ – autorsko izdanje 2015.
- “Paris – ili zalud je razapinjati Krista/ Paride - È inutile crocifiggere Cristo” - „Providenca“ 2015 i
- „Ogledi“ – „Providenca“ 2016,
- “Banka” – “Narodno pozorište RS” – 2017 i
- “Vjetrovi/ I Venti” – “Providenca” – 2017.

Babylonian Strumpet

Your Grail
was built upon your
avidity and
wantonness
You who are willing to
suffer the chastisement
due to the feebleness
of others
trusting in the righteous' shroud
speak:
"Drink, your blood
and wine
my shame is
peerless
without my ignominy.
I am an outcast
for I wanted it to be;
I wore
crowns duly.
My Grail has been
made."

Upon Looking In The Mirror

The shame shrouded with
A tear on
The jester's
Face
Awakens holiness
On the trail and
Deadlock
Which alters
The tremor
Into laughter
Although the overshadow
Withstands
The rays
Seeking one another
And the hint of which
Was dreamy
Under the gown
To which they
Bowed
In vain…

The Healing

For the well
In his dreams
While it strides down
The score
In the form of
The drunken
Ink which
Is an excuse
To the Maestro through its
Thoughtfulness
Shows the way
Even though at
The horizon
In this hourglass
There is no grain
Nor rudder
Nor stern
Only the anchor
A knot around the neck…

T. Ashok Chakravarthy

Dr. Ashok Chakravarthy, Poet, India, is composing poetry for over 25 years and of the 2000 poems composed, nearly 1600 poems appeared in various magazines, journals, anthologies, newspapers etc. in over 90 countries. His 6 volumes of poetry viz., *Charismata of Poesie, Chariot of Musings, Serene Thoughts, Twinkles, Reflections, Altitudes* received wide readership acclaim. His poetry is aimed to promote universal peace, environment awareness, Children rights protection etc. He was adjudged with several international awards, viz., Universal Peace Ambassador, Love Ambassador, Asian Who's Who & conferred with 4 doctorates and received 'First Laureate of the World of Literature 2017' on the Independence of KAZAKHSTAN.

http://peacefromharmony.org/?cat=en_c&key=286

www.upli-wcp.org/poet-and-poems-for-the-month-of-may-2017/

Unfading Memories

Like a welcome shower
Dousing the heat of a sultry summer,
Like a bright shining sun
Piercing the clouds of a mid-monsoon,
Like the crescent moon in the sly
Peeping through the star-lit cloudy sky,
Unfading memories of childhood
Traverse all through life's varied mood.

Grown from the cozy lap of mother
Through the secured hands of father,
The whirl-pools of advancing age,
Leave foot-prints at every life's stage.
Those colorful and naughty chosen ranks
Those ever playful and childish pranks,
Become more treasured, as age advances
Till fag end, they remain top memories.
While innocence reigns the days
Future, looming large in many a way,
Yes, whatever be the outcome
Facing any type of storm that comes;
One should not ignore basic morals
To experience and tame life's hassles
For leading a content-filled life
Bearing and sharing, pain and grief.

Survival And Revival

Entangled in the snares of materialistic world
Passing the day-to-day life under 'desires sword';
The consequences of passions often entangle us
Reminding, life is not a mere destination for bliss.

Outwardly, we are not what we really are
But inwardly we possess some invisible power;
Betwixt these indistinguishable dualities,
There exists God, with inconceivable realities.

How mighty His Hand is, How Graceful His eyes
Crowning the day with light, He mesmerizes;
Adorning the night sky with moon and stars,
It's He, Who wields control over universe and skies.

Most mysterious are ways of God, The Creator
Most Benevolent are the Eyes of God, The Savior;
Under whose merciful eyes we act on life's stage
Unaware, we are caught in a pre-destined cage.

Yes, moment after moment of our very survival
Depend on the "Ocean of Mercy's" bestowal;
God! The Invisible but Supremely Powerful
Runs the show of "Every Survival and Revival".

Till The Last Breathe

Thoughts, pave a way for new desires
Desires in turn transform into dreams;
Childhood, as it pierced through years
Dreamed of youth, to dispel life's fears.

Days were delightful with ever-new cheer
Youthful days soared like a brimming river,
Day and night, the thirst for love surged
Boundless dreams one after another budged.

The relentless and unquenched love-thirst
At last pierced deep into the heart of heart;
The phase of a new transformation began
The youthful phase tried to hold, but in vain.

Another spell of dream for riches and luxuries
Unfolded with a new vigor and new worries;
The eye of wisdom awakened to peep into life
And realized, dreams often invite grief into life.

For God has bestowed us with a valuable 'life'
It's better to feel content to keep at bay; grief.
Short-lived and unfulfilled dreams are perilous
For; till the last breathe they hunt and hurt us.

Inner Child Press

News

We are so excited to announce the New and upcoming books of some of our Poetry Posse authors.

On the following pages we present to you ...

Jackie Davis Allen

Gail Weston Shazor

hülya n. yılmaz

Nizar Sartawi

Faleeha Hassan

Caroline 'Ceri' Nazareno

William S. Peters, Sr.

Coming January of 2019

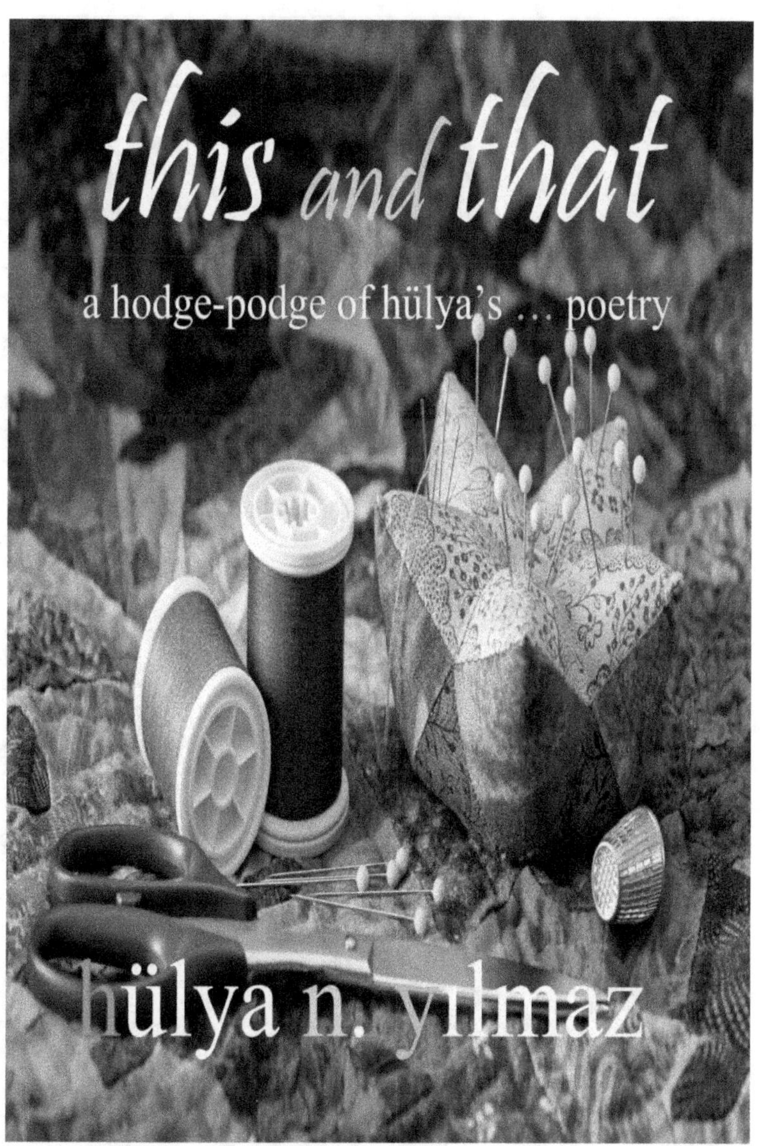
this and that
a hodge-podge of hülya's … poetry
hülya n. yılmaz

Coming January of 2019

No Illusions
Through the Looking Glass
Jackie Davis Allen

Now Available at

www.innerchildpress.com

Dark Side
of the
Moon
Jackie Davis Allen

Now Available at

www.innerchildpress.com

Lies
My
Grandfathers
Told
Me
Gail Weston Shazor

Now Available at

www.innerchildpress.com

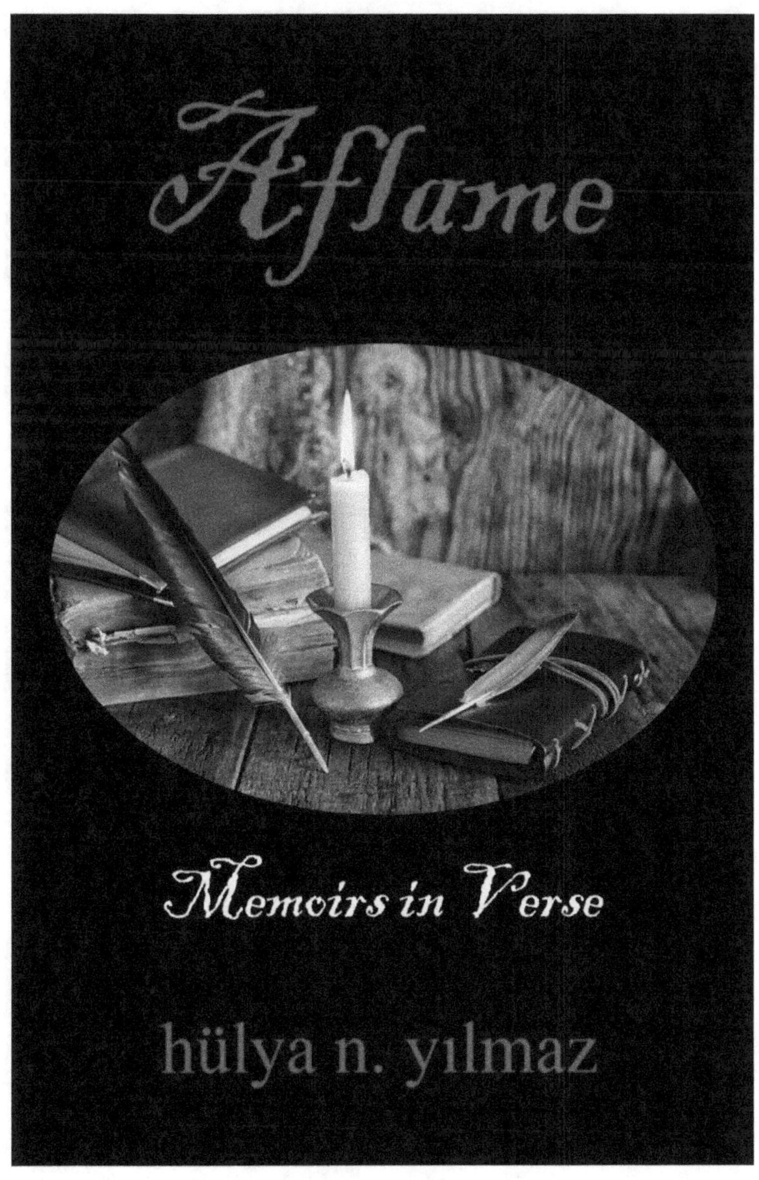
Aflame
Memoirs in Verse
hülya n. yılmaz

Now Available at

www.innerchildpress.com

My Shadow
Nizar Sartawi

Now Available at

www.innerchildpress.com

Mass Graves
Faleeha Hassan

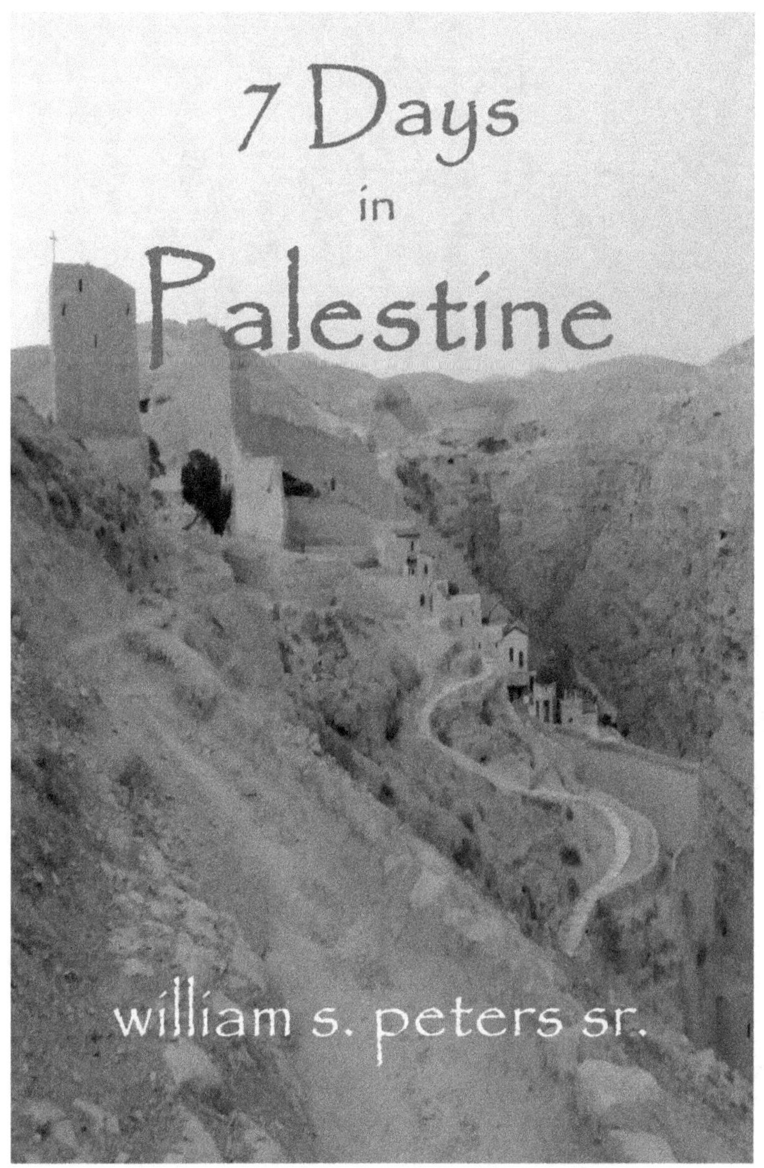
7 Days
in
Palestine
william s. peters sr.

Now Available at

www.innerchildpress.com

inner child press
presents
Tunisia My Love
william s. peters, sr.

Coming in December of 2018

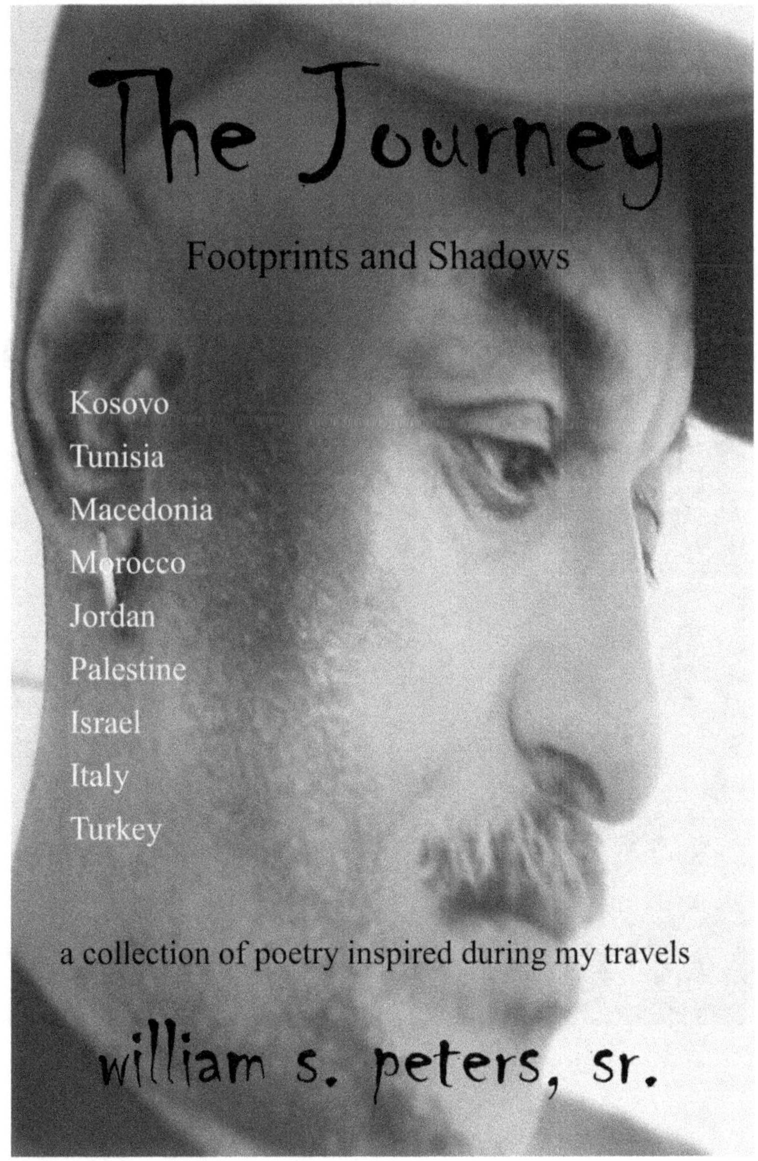
The Journey
Footprints and Shadows
Kosovo
Tunisia
Macedonia
Morocco
Jordan
Palestine
Israel
Italy
Turkey
a collection of poetry inspired during my travels
william s. peters, sr.

Now Available at

www.innerchildpress.com

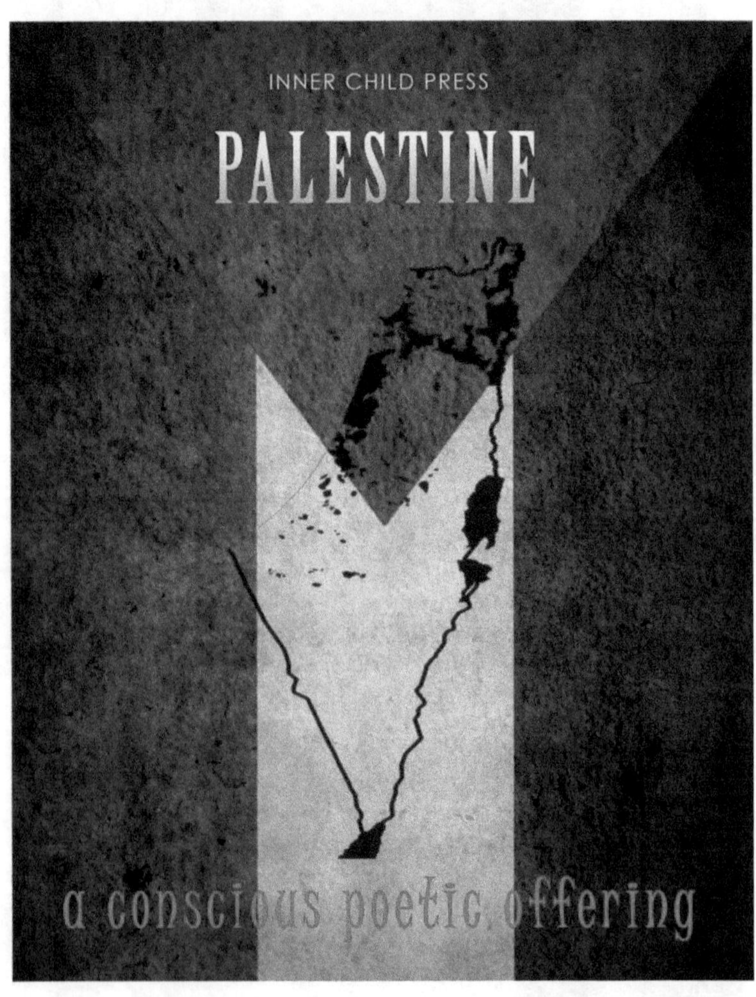
INNER CHILD PRESS
PALESTINE
a conscious poetic offering

Now Available at

www.innerchildpress.com

INNER CHILD PRESS
WORLD HEALING
WORLD PEACE
2018
A Poetry Anthology for Humanity

Now Available at

www.innerchildpress.com

INNER CHILD PRESS
THIS IS WHY I
SLEEP
william s. peters sr.

Now Available at

www.innerchildpress.com

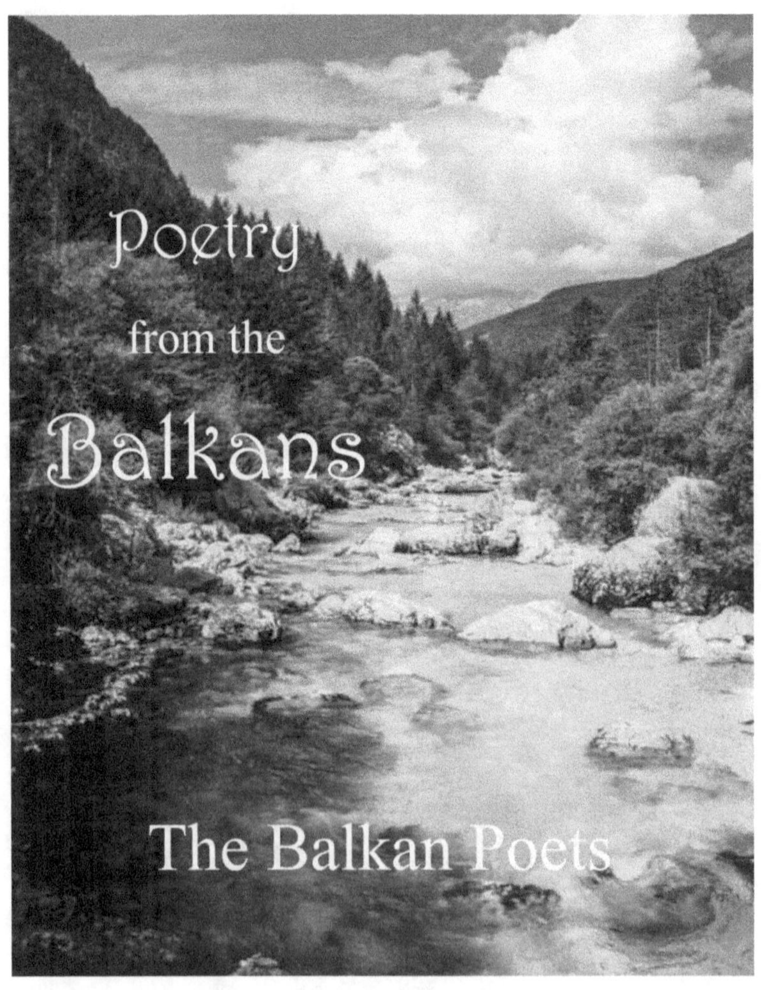
Poetry
from the
Balkans
The Balkan Poets

Other

Anthological

works from

Inner Child Press, ltd.

www.innerchildpress.com

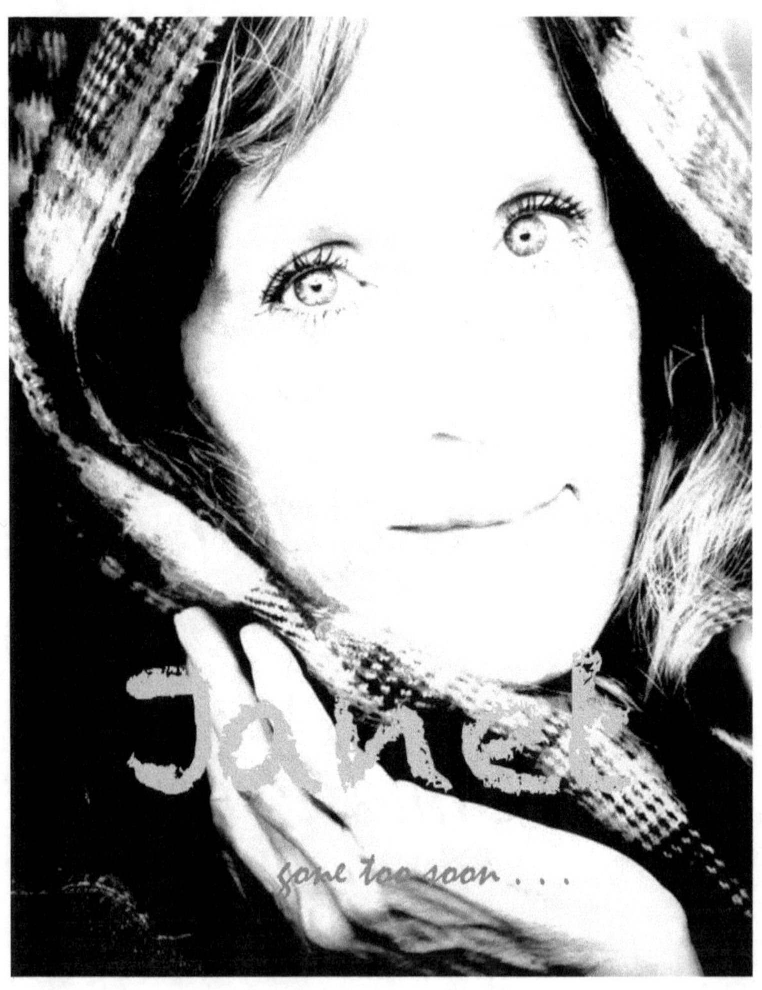
Janet
gone too soon . . .

Now Available

www.innerchildpress.com/janet-p-caldwell.php

INNER CHILD PRESS
WORLD HEALING
WORLD PEACE
2018
A Poetry Anthology for Humanity

Now Available

www.worldhealingworldpeacepoetry.com

INNER CHILD PRESS
World Healing
World Peace
A Poetry Anthology 2014
Volume 1
INNER CHILD PRESS
World Healing
World Peace
A Poetry Anthology 2014
Volume 2

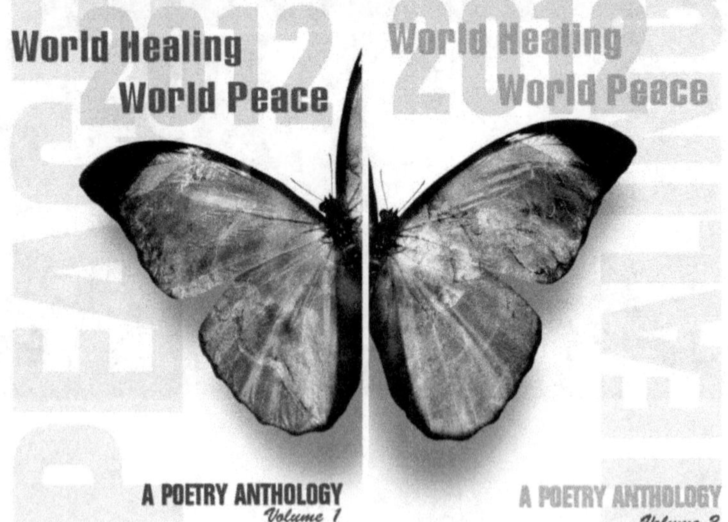
2012
World Healing
World Peace
A POETRY ANTHOLOGY
Volume 1
2012
World Healing
World Peace
A POETRY ANTHOLOGY
Volume 2

Now Available

www.worldhealingworldpeacepoetry.com

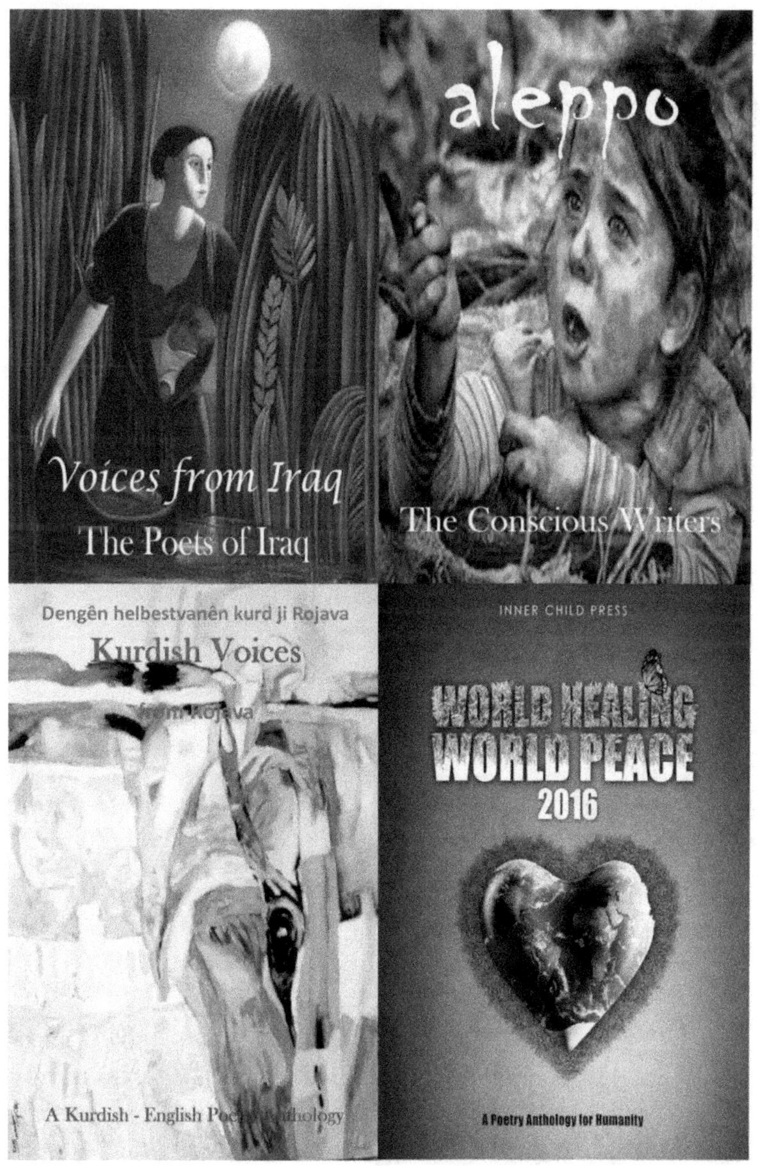
Voices from Iraq
The Poets of Iraq
aleppo
The Conscious Writers
Dengên helbestvanên kurd ji Rojava
Kurdish Voices
A Kurdish - English Poetry Anthology
INNER CHILD PRESS
WORLD HEALING
WORLD PEACE
2016
A Poetry Anthology for Humanity

Now Available

www.innerchildpress.com/anthologies

Mandela

The Man
His Life
Its Meaning
Our Words

Poetry . . . Commentary & Stories

The Anthological Writers

A GATHERING OF WORDS

POETRY & COMMENTARY

FOR

TRAYVON MARTIN

INNER CHILD PRESS
BLACK MALE-D
The Black Male Writers
Imam Jamil Abdullah Al-Amin
aka H. Rap Brown

Now Available

www.innerchildpress.com/anthologies

Hot Summer Nights...
Hot Summer Nights... 2013
A Collection of Erotic Poetry, Prose & Story
by the The Erotic Writers
INNER CHILD PRESS
PRESENTS
Hot Summer Nights... 2014
A COLLECTION OF EROTIC POETRY, PROSE & STORIES
poetry . . . prose & stories of love
The Love Writers

Now Available

www.innerchildpress.com/anthologies

Inner Child Press Anthologies

Janet

healing through words
Poetry ... Prose ... Prayer ... Stories

a
Poetically
Spoken
Anthology
volume I
Collector's Edition

The Poetry Posse
Presents
an anthology
of
Love
The Poetry Posse 2016

Now Available

www.innerchildpress.com/anthologies

Inner Child Press Anthologies

i want my
PoEtRy
to . . .
a collection of the Voices of Many inspired by . . .
Monte Smith

a collection of the Voices of Many inspired by . . .

Monte Smith

i want my

PoEtRy

to . . .

volume II

i want my

PoEtRy

to . . . volume 3

a collection of the Voices of Many inspired by . . .

Monte Smith

11 Words

(9 lines . . .)

for those who are challenged

an anthology of Poetry inspired by . . .

Poetry Dancer

Now Available

www.innerchildpress.com/anthologies

The Year of the Poet
January 2014
The Poetry Posse
Jamie Bond
Gail Weston Shazor
Albert 'Infinite' Carrasco
Siddartha Beth Pierce
Janet P. Caldwell
June 'Bugg' Barefield
Debbie M. Allen
Tony Henninger
Joe DaVerbal Minddancer
Robert Gibbons
Neetu Wali
Shareef Abdur-Rasheed
William S. Peters, Sr.
Carnation
Our January Feature
Terri L. Johnson

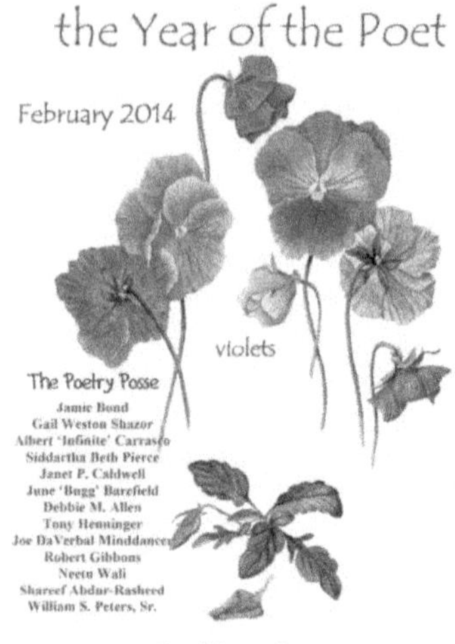
the Year of the Poet
February 2014
violets
The Poetry Posse
Jamie Bond
Gail Weston Shazor
Albert 'Infinite' Carrasco
Siddartha Beth Pierce
Janet P. Caldwell
June 'Bugg' Barefield
Debbie M. Allen
Tony Henninger
Joe DaVerbal Minddancer
Robert Gibbons
Neetu Wali
Shareef Abdur-Rasheed
William S. Peters, Sr.
Our February Features
Teresa E. Gallion & Robert Gibson

March 2014
The Poetry Posse
Our March Featured Poets
Alicia C. Cooper & hülya yılmaz

the Year of the Poet
April 2014
The Poetry Posse
Our April Featured Poets
Fahredin Shehu
Martina Reisz Newberry
Justin Blackburn
Monte Smith
Sweet Pea
celebrating international poetry month

Now Available

www.innerchildpress.com/the-year-of-the-poet

Inner Child Press Anthologies

the year of the poet
May 2014
May's Featured Poets
ReeCee
Joski the Poet
Shannon Stanton
Dedicated To our Children
The Poetry Posse
Lily of the Valley
the Year of the Poet
June 2014
Love & Relationship
Rose
The Poetry Posse
Jamie Bond
Gail Weston Shazor
Albert 'Infinite' Carrasco
Siddartha Beth Pierce
Janet P. Caldwell
June 'Bugg' Barefield
Debbie M. Allen
Tony Henninger
Joe DaVerbal Minddancer
Robert Gibbons
Neetu Wali
Shareef Abdur-Rasheed
Kimberly Burnham
William S. Peters, Sr.
June's Featured Poets
Shanelle McLin
Jacqueline D. E. Kennedy
Abraham N. Benjamin
The Year of the Poet
July 2014
July Feature Poets
Christene A. V. Williams
Dr. John R. Strum
Kolade Olanrewaju Freedom
The Poetry Posse
Jamie Bond
Gail Weston Shazor
June 'Bugg' Barefield
Debbie M. Allen
Tony Henninger
Joe DaVerbal Minddancer
Robert Gibbons
Neetu Wali
Shareef Abdur-Rasheed
Kimberly Burnham
William S. Peters, Sr.
Lotus
Asian Flower of the Month
The Year of the Poet
August 2014
Gladiolus
The Poetry Posse
Jamie Bond
Gail Weston Shazor
Albert 'Infinite' Carrasco
Siddartha Beth Pierce
Janet P. Caldwell
June 'Bugg' Barefield
Debbie M. Allen
Tony Henninger
Joe DaVerbal Minddancer
Robert Gibbons
Neetu Wali
Shareef Abdur-Rasheed
Kimberly Burnham
William S. Peters, Sr.
August Feature Poets
Ann White * Rosalind Cherry * Sheila Jenkins

Now Available

www.innerchildpress.com/the-year-of-the-poet

The Year of the Poet
September 2014
Aster
Morning-Glory
September Feature Poets
Florence Malone * Keith Alan Hamilton
The Poetry Posse
Jamie Bond * Gail Weston Shazor * Albert 'Infinite' Carrasco * Siddartha Beth Pierce
Janet P. Caldwell * June 'Bugg' Barefield * Debbie M. Allen * Tony Henninger
Joe DaVerbal Minddancer * Robert Gibbons * Neetu Wali * Shareef Abdur-Rasheed
Kimberly Burnham * William S. Peters, Sr.

The Year of the Poet
October 2014
Red Poppy
The Poetry Posse
Jamie Bond * Gail Weston Shazor * Albert 'Infinite' Carrasco * Siddartha Beth Pierce
Janet P. Caldwell * June 'Bugg' Barefield * Debbie M. Allen * Tony Henninger
Joe DaVerbal Minddancer * Robert Gibbons * Neetu Wali * Shareef Abdur-Rasheed
Kimberly Burnham * William S. Peters, Sr.
October Feature Poets
Ceri Naz * Rajendra Padhi * Elizabeth Castillo

The Year of the Poet
November 2014
Chrysanthemum
The Poetry Posse
November Feature Poets
Jocelyn Mosman * Jackie Allen * James Moore * Neville Hiatt

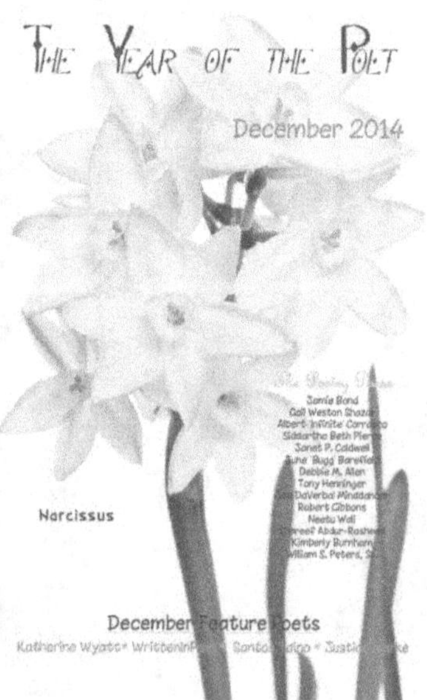
The Year of the Poet
December 2014
Narcissus

Now Available

www.innerchildpress.com/the-year-of-the-poet

The Year of the Poet II
January 2015
Garnet
The Poetry Posse
Jamie Bond
Gail Weston Shazor
Albert 'Infinite' Carrasco
Siddartha Beth Pierce
Janet P. Caldwell
Tony Henninger
Joe DaVerbal Minddancer
Robert Gibbons
Neetu Wali
Shareef Abdur - Rasheed
Kimberly Burnham
Ann White
Keith Alan Hamilton
Katherine Wyatt
Fahredin Shehu
Hülya N. Yilmaz
Teresa E. Gallion
Jackie Allen
William S. Peters, Sr.
January Feature Poets
Bismay Mohanti * Jen Walls * Eric Judah

THE YEAR OF THE POET II

February 2015

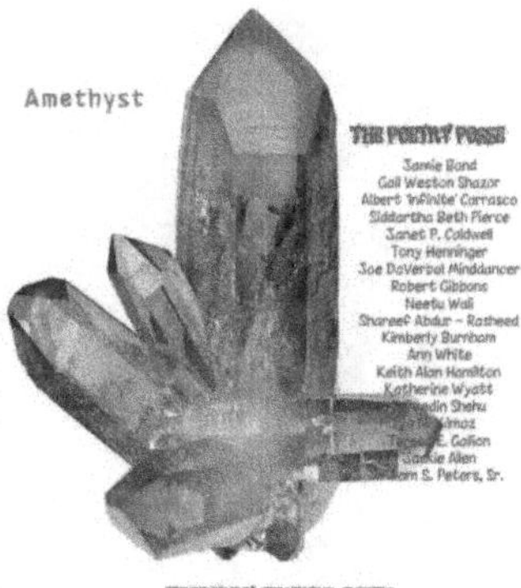
Amethyst
THE POETRY POSSE
Jamie Bond
Gail Weston Shazor
Albert 'Infinite' Carrasco
Siddartha Beth Pierce
Janet P. Caldwell
Tony Henninger
Joe DaVerbal Minddancer
Robert Gibbons
Neetu Wali
Shareef Abdur - Rasheed
Kimberly Burnham
Ann White
Keith Alan Hamilton
Katherine Wyatt

FEBRUARY FEATURE POETS

Iram Fatima * Bob McNeil * Kerstin Centervall

The Year of the Poet II

March 2015

Our Featured Poets

Heung Sook * Anthony Arnold * Alicia Poland

Bloodstone

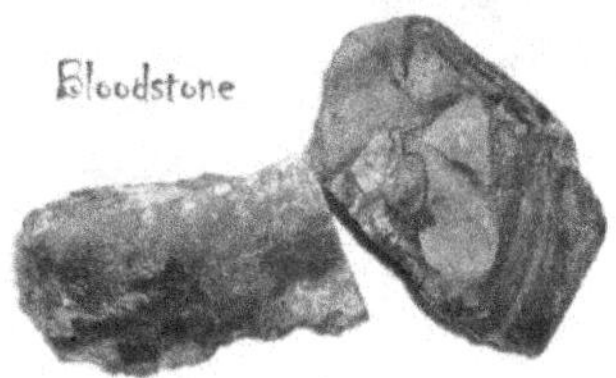

The Poetry Posse 2015

Jamie Bond * Gail Weston Shazor * Albert 'Infinite' Carrasco
Siddartha Beth Pierce * Janet P. Caldwell * Tony Henninger
Joe DaVerbal Minddancer * Neetu Wali * Shareef Abdur – Rasheed
Kimberly Burnham * Ann White * Keith Alan Hamilton
Katherine Wyatt * Fahredin Shehu * Hülya N. Yilmaz
Teresa E. Gallion * Jackie Allen * William S. Peters, Sr.

The Year of the Poet II
April 2015
Celebrating International Poetry Month
Our Featured Poets
Raja Williams * Dennis Ferado * Laure Charazac
Diamonds
The Poetry Posse 2015
Jamie Bond * Gail Weston Shazor * Albert 'Infinite' Carrasco
Siddartha Beth Pierce * Janet P. Caldwell * Tony Henninger
Joe DaVerbal Minddancer * Neetu Wali * Shareef Abdur – Rasheed
Kimberly Burnham * Ann White * Keith Alan Hamilton
Katherine Wyatt * Fahredin Shehu * Hülya N. Yilmaz
Teresa E. Gallion * Jackie Allen * William S. Peters, Sr.

Now Available

www.innerchildpress.com/the-year-of-the-poet

Inner Child Press Anthologies

The Year of the Poet II
May 2015
May's Featured Poets
Geri Algeri
Emeralds
The Poetry Posse 2015
Joe DaVerbal Minddancer * Neetu Wali * Shareef Abdur – Rasheed
Kimberly Burnham * Ann White * Keith Alan Hamilton
Katherine Wyatt * Fahredin Shehu * Hülya N. Yılmaz
Teresa E. Gallion * Jackie Allen * William S. Peters, Sr.

The Year of the Poet II

June 2015

June's Featured Poets

Anahit Arustamyan * Yvette D. Murrell * Regina A. Walker

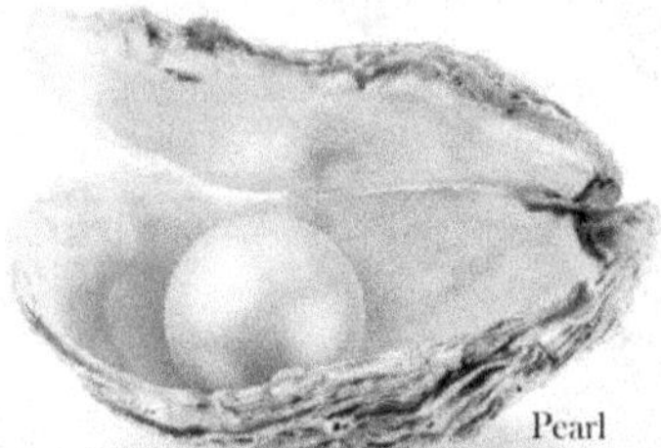

Pearl

The Poetry Posse 2015

Jamie Bond * Gail Weston Shazor * Albert 'Infinite' Carrasco
Siddartha Beth Pierce * Janet P. Caldwell * Tony Henninger
Joe DaVerbal Minddancer * Neetu Wali * Shareef Abdur – Rasheed
Kimberly Burnham * Ann White * Keith Alan Hamilton
Katherine Wyatt * Fahredin Shehu * Hülya N. Yılmaz
Teresa E. Gallion * Jackie Allen * William S. Peters, Sr.

The Year of the Poet II

July 2015

The Featured Poets for July 2015

Abhik Shome * Christina Neal * Robert Neal

Rubies

The Poetry Posse 2015

Jamie Bond * Gail Weston Shazor * Albert 'Infinite' Carrasco
Siddartha Beth Pierce * Janet P. Caldwell * Tony Henninger
Joe DaVerbal Minddancer * Neetu Wali * Shareef Abdur – Rasheed
Kimberly Burnham * Ann White * Keith Alan Hamilton
Katherine Wyatt * Fahredin Shehu * Hülya N. Yılmaz
Teresa E. Gallion * Jackie Allen * William S. Peters, Sr.

The Year of the Poet II

August 2015

Peridot

Featured Poets

Gayle Howell
Ann Chalasz
Christopher Schultz

The Poetry Posse 2015

Jamie Bond * Gail Weston Shazor * Albert 'Infinite' Carrasco
Siddartha Beth Pierce * Janet P. Caldwell * Tony Henninger
Joe DaVerbal Minddancer * Neetu Wali * Shareef Abdur – Rasheed
Kimberly Burnham * Ann White * Keith Alan Hamilton
Katherine Wyatt * Fahredin Shehu * Hülya N. Yılmaz
Teresa E. Gallion * Jackie Allen * William S. Peters, Sr.

Now Available

www.innerchildpress.com/the-year-of-the-poet

Inner Child Press Anthologies

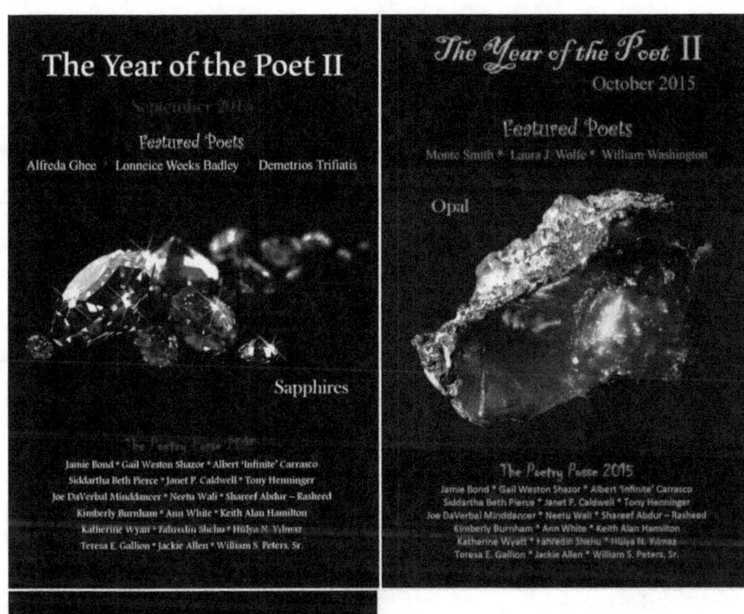

The Year of the Poet II
Featured Poets
Alfreda Ghee
Lonneice Weeks Badley
Demetrios Trifiatis
Sapphires
The Year of the Poet II
October 2015
Featured Poets
Opal
The Poetry Posse 2015
Jamie Bond * Gail Weston Shazor * Albert 'Infinite' Carrasco
Siddartha Beth Pierce * Janet P. Caldwell * Tony Henninger
Joe DaVerbal Minddancer * Neetu Wali * Shareef Abdur – Rasheed
Kimberly Burnham * Ann White * Keith Alan Hamilton
Katherine Wyatt * Fahredin Shehu * Hülya N. Yilmaz
Teresa E. Gallion * Jackie Allen * William S. Peters, Sr.

The Year of the Poet II
November 2015
Featured Poets
Alan W. Jankowski
Bismay Mohanty
James Moore
Topaz
The Poetry Posse 2015
Jamie Bond * Gail Weston Shazor * Albert 'Infinite' Carrasco
Siddartha Beth Pierce * Janet P. Caldwell * Tony Henninger
Joe DaVerbal Minddancer * Neetu Wali * Shareef Abdur – Rasheed
Kimberly Burnham * Ann White * Keith Alan Hamilton
Katherine Wyatt * Fahredin Shehu * Hülya N. Yilmaz
Teresa E. Gallion * Jackie Allen * William S. Peters, Sr.

The Year of the Poet II
December 2015

Featured Poets
Kerione Bryan * Michelle Joan Barulich * Neville Hiatt

Turquoise

The Poetry Posse 2015
Jamie Bond * Gail Weston Shazor * Albert 'Infinite' Carrasco
Siddartha Beth Pierce * Janet P. Caldwell * Tony Henninger
Joe DaVerbal Minddancer * Neetu Wali * Shareef Abdur – Rasheed
Kimberly Burnham * Ann White * Keith Alan Hamilton
Katherine Wyatt * Fahredin Shehu * Hülya N. Yilmaz
Teresa E. Gallion * Jackie Allen * William S. Peters, Sr.

Now Available

www.innerchildpress.com/the-year-of-the-poet

Inner Child Press Anthologies

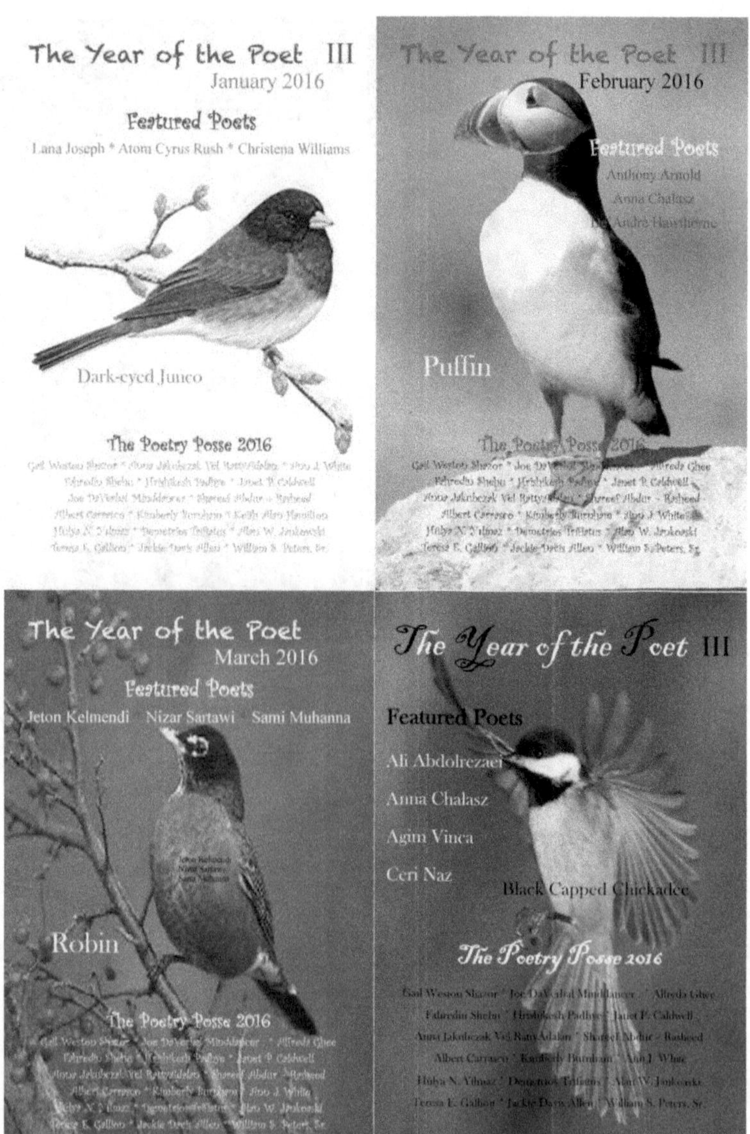
The Year of the Poet III
January 2016
Featured Poets
Lana Joseph * Atom Cyrus Rush * Christena Williams
Dark-eyed Junco
The Poetry Posse 2016
The Year of the Poet III
February 2016
Featured Poets
Anthony Arnold
Anna Chalasz
Dr. André Hawthorne
Puffin
The Poetry Posse 2016
The Year of the Poet
March 2016
Featured Poets
Jeton Kelmendi Nizar Sartawi Sami Muhanna
Robin
The Poetry Posse 2016
The Year of the Poet III
Featured Poets
Ali Abdolrezaei
Anna Chalasz
Agim Vinca
Ceri Naz
Black Capped Chickadee
The Poetry Posse 2016
celebrating international poetry month

Now Available

www.innerchildpress.com/the-year-of-the-poet

Inner Child Press Anthologies

The Year of the Poet
May 2016
Bob Strum
Barbara Allan
D.L. Davis
Oriole
The Year of the Poet III
June 2016
Featured Poets
Qibrije Demiri- Frangu
Naime Beqiraj
Faleeha Hassan
Bedri Zyberaj
Black Necked Stilt
The Poetry Posse 2016
Iram Fatima 'Ashi'
Langley Shazor
Jody Doty
Emilia T. Davis
Indigo Bunting
The Poetry Posse 2016
The Year of the Poet III
August 2016
Featured Poets
Anita Dash
Irena Jovanovic
Malgorzata Gouluda
Painted Bunting
The Poetry Posse 2016

Now Available

www.innerchildpress.com/the-year-of-the-poet

The Year of the Poet III
September 2016
Featured Poets
Simone Weber
Abhijit Sen
Eunice Barbara C. Novio
The Poetry Posse 2016
The Year of the Poet III
October 2016
Featured Poets
The Year of the Poet III
November 2016
Featured Poets
Rosemary Burns
Robin Ouzman Hislop
Lonneice Weeks-Badley
Northern Cardinal
The Poetry Posse 2016
Gail Weston Shazor * Caroline Nazareno * Jen Walls
Nizar Sartawi * Janet P. Caldwell * Alfreda Ghee
Joe DaVerbal Minddancer * Shareef Abdur – Rasheed
Albert Carrasco * Kimberly Burnham * Elizabeth Castillo
Hülya N. Yılmaz * Demetrios Trifiatis * Alan W. Jankowski
Teresa E. Gallion * Jackie Davis Allen * William S. Peters, Sr.
The Year of the Poet III
December 2016
Featured Poets
Samih Masoud
Mountassir Aziz Bien
Abdulkadir Musa
Rough Legged Hawk
The Poetry Posse 2016

Now Available

www.innerchildpress.com/the-year-of-the-poet

Inner Child Press Anthologies

The Year of the Poet IV
May 2017

The Flowering Dogwood Tree

Featured Poets
Kallisa Powell
Aličja Maria Kuberska
Fethi Sassi

The Poetry Posse 2017

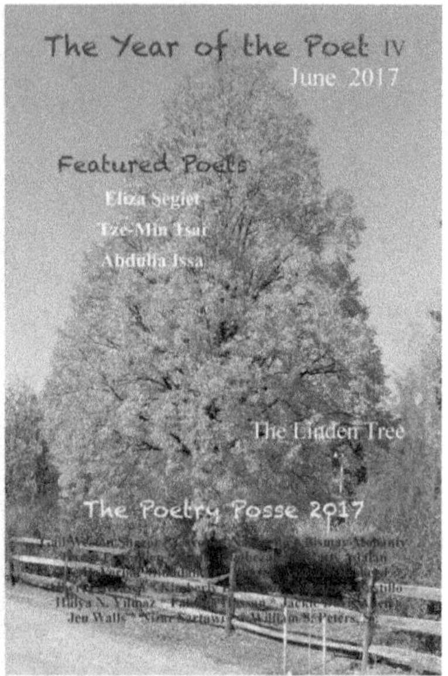

The Year of the Poet IV
June 2017
Featured Poets
Eliza Segiet
Tze-Min Tsai
Abdulla Issa
The Linden Tree
The Poetry Posse 2017

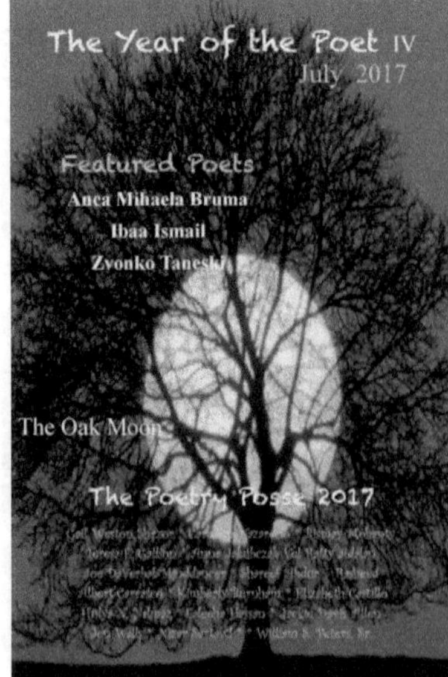

The Year of the Poet IV
July 2017
Featured Poets
Anca Mihaela Bruma
Ibaa Ismail
Zvonko Taneski
The Oak Moon
The Poetry Posse 2017

The Year of the Poet IV
August 2017

Jonathan Aquino
Kitty Hsu
Langley Shazor
The Hazelnut Tree
The Poetry Posse 2017

Now Available

www.innerchildpress.com/the-year-of-the-poet

Inner Child Press Anthologies

The Year of the Poet IV
September 2017

Featured Poets

Martina Reisz Newberry

Ameer Nassir

Christine Fulco Neal

Robert Neal

The Elm Tree

The Poetry Posse 2017

Gail Weston Shazor * Caroline Nazareno * Bismay Mohanty
Teresa E. Gallion * Anna Jakubczak Vel Ratty Adalan
Joe DaVerbal Minddancer * Shareef Abdur – Rasheed
Albert Carrasco * Kimberly Burnham * Elizabeth Castillo
Hülya N. Yilmaz * Faleeha Hassan * Jackie Davis Allen
Jen Walls * Nizar Sartawi * * William S. Peters, Sr.

The Year of the Poet IV
October 2017

Featured Poets

Ahmed Abu Saleem

Nedal Al-Qaeim

Sadeddin Shahin

The Black Walnut Tree

The Poetry Posse 2017

Gail Weston Shazor * Caroline Nazareno * Bismay Mohanty
Teresa E. Gallion * Anna Jakubczak Vel Ratty Adalan
Joe DaVerbal Minddancer * Shareef Abdur – Rasheed
Albert Carrasco * Kimberly Burnham * Elizabeth Castillo
Hülya N. Yilmaz * Faleeha Hassan * Jackie Davis Allen
Jen Walls * Nizar Sartawi * * William S. Peters, Sr.

The Year of the Poet IV
November 2017

Featured Poets

Kay Peters

Alfreda D. Ghee

Gabriella Garofalo

Rosemary Cappello

The Tree of Life

The Poetry Posse 2017

Gail Weston Shazor * Caroline Nazareno * Bismay Mohanty
Teresa E. Gallion * Anna Jakubczak Vel Ratty Adalan
Joe DaVerbal Minddancer * Shareef Abdur – Rasheed
Albert Carrasco * Kimberly Burnham * Elizabeth Castillo
Hülya N. Yilmaz * Faleeha Hassan * Jackie Davis Allen
Jen Walls * Nizar Sartawi * William S. Peters, Sr.

The Year of the Poet IV
December 2017

Featured Poets

Justice Clarke

Mariel M. Pabroa

Kiley Brown

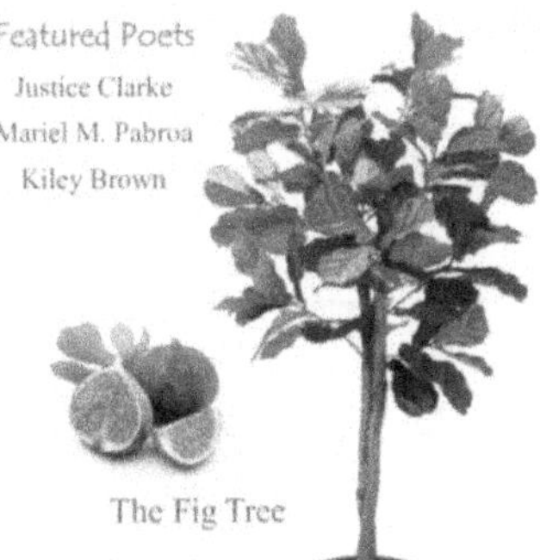

The Fig Tree

The Poetry Posse 2017

Gail Weston Shazor * Caroline Nazareno * Bismay Mohanty
Teresa E. Gallion * Anna Jakubczak Vel Ratty Adalan
Joe DaVerbal Minddancer * Shareef Abdur – Rasheed
Albert Carrasco * Kimberly Burnham * Elizabeth Castillo
Hülya N. Yilmaz * Faleeha Hassan * Jackie Davis Allen
Jen Walls * Nizar Sartawi * William S. Peters, Sr.

Now Available

www.innerchildpress.com/the-year-of-the-poet

Inner Child Press Anthologies

The Year of the Poet V
January 2018
Featured Poets
Iyad Shamasnah
Yasmeen Hamzeh
Ali Abdolrezaei
Aksum
The Poetry Posse 2018
The Year of the Poet V
February 2018
Sabean
Featured Poets
Muhammad Azram
Anna Szawracka
Abhilipsa Kuanar
Aanika Aery
The Poetry Posse 2018
Gail Weston Shazor * Caroline Nazareno * Tezmin Ition Tsai
Hülya N. Yılmaz * Faleeha Hassan * Jackie Davis Allen
Teresa E. Gallion * Anna Jakubczak Vel Ratty Adalan
Alicja Maria Kuberska * Shareef Abdur – Rasheed
Kimberly Burnham * Elizabeth Castillo
Nizar Sartawi * William S. Peters, Sr.
The Year of the Poet V
March 2018
Featured Poets
Iram Fatima 'Ashi'
Cassandra Swan
Jaleel Khazaal
Shazia Zaman
Mexico
Cuba
Belize
Jamaica
Haiti
Puerto Rico
Guatemala
Honduras
El Salvador
Nicaragua
Costa Rica
Panama
Colombia
Caribbean
&
Middle America
The Poetry Posse 2018
Gail Weston Shazor * Nizar Sartawi * Hülya N. Yılmaz
Jackie Davis Allen * Caroline 'Ceri' Nazareno
Alicja Maria Kuberska * Teresa E. Gallion
Faleeha Hassan * Shareef Abdur – Rasheed
Kimberly Burnham * Elizabeth Castillo
Tezmin Ition Tsai * William S. Peters, Sr
The Year of the Poet V
April 2018
Featured Poets
The Nez Perce

Now Available

www.innerchildpress.com/the-year-of-the-poet

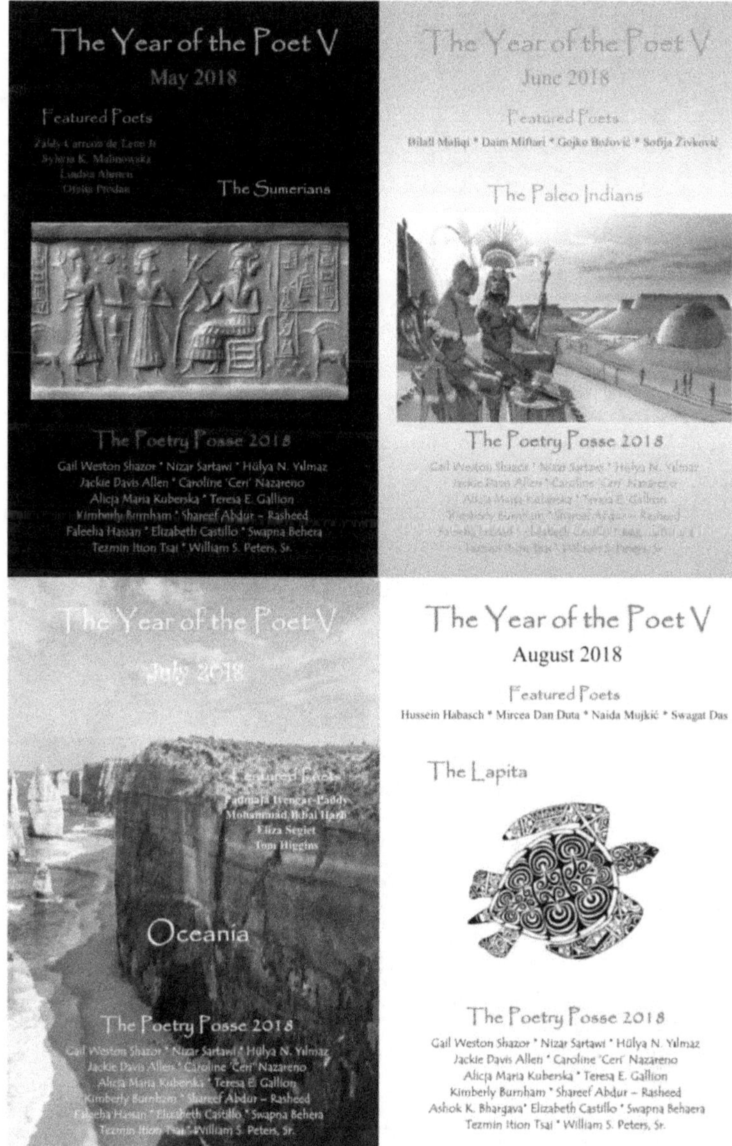

The Year of the Poet V
May 2018
Featured Poets
The Sumerians
The Poetry Posse 2018
Gail Weston Shazor * Nizar Sartawi * Hülya N. Yılmaz
Jackie Davis Allen * Caroline 'Ceri' Nazareno
Alicja Maria Kuberska * Teresa E. Gallion
Kimberly Burnham * Shareef Abdur – Rasheed
Faleeha Hassan * Elizabeth Castillo * Swapna Behera
Tezmin Ition Tsai * William S. Peters, Sr.
The Year of the Poet V
June 2018
Featured Poets
Bilall Maliqi * Daim Miftari * Gojko Božović * Sofija Živković
The Paleo Indians
The Poetry Posse 2018
The Year of the Poet V
July 2018
Oceania
The Poetry Posse 2018
Gail Weston Shazor * Nizar Sartawi * Hülya N. Yılmaz
Jackie Davis Allen * Caroline 'Ceri' Nazareno
Alicja Maria Kuberska * Teresa E. Gallion
Kimberly Burnham * Shareef Abdur – Rasheed
Faleeha Hassan * Elizabeth Castillo * Swapna Behera
Tezmin Ition Tsai * William S. Peters, Sr.
The Year of the Poet V
August 2018
Featured Poets
Hussein Habasch * Mircea Dan Duta * Naida Mujkić * Swagat Das
The Lapita
The Poetry Posse 2018
Gail Weston Shazor * Nizar Sartawi * Hülya N. Yılmaz
Jackie Davis Allen * Caroline 'Ceri' Nazareno
Alicja Maria Kuberska * Teresa E. Gallion
Kimberly Burnham * Shareef Abdur – Rasheed
Ashok K. Bhargava * Elizabeth Castillo * Swapna Behaera
Tezmin Ition Tsai * William S. Peters, Sr.

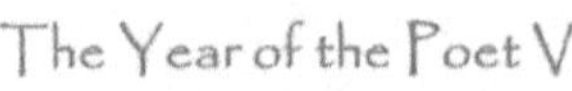
The Year of the Poet V

September 2018

The Aztecs & Incas

Featured Poets

The Poetry Posse 2018

The Year of the Poet V
October 2018
Featured Poets
Alicia Minjarez * Lonneice Weeks-Badley
Lopamudra Mishra * Abdelwahed Souayah
Bengali
The Poetry Posse 2018
Gail Weston Shazor * Nizar Sartawi * Hülya N. Yılmaz
Jackie Davis Allen * Caroline 'Ceri' Nazareno
Alicja Maria Kuberska * Teresa E. Gallion
Kimberly Burnham * Shareef Abdur – Rasheed
Ashok K. Bhargava * Elizabeth Castillo * Swapna Behera
Tezmin Ition Tsai * William S. Peters, Sr.

The Year of the Poet V

November 2018

Featured Poets

Michelle Joan Barulich * Monsif Beroual
Krystyna Konecka * Nassira Nezzar

The Poetry Posse 2018

The Year of the Poet V
December 2018
Featured Poets
Rose Terranova Cirigliano
Joanna Kalinowska
Sokolović Emin
Dr. T. Ashok Chakravarthy
The Maori
Gail Weston Shazor * Nizar Sartawi * Hülya N. Yılmaz
Jackie Davis Allen * Caroline 'Ceri' Nazareno
Alicja Maria Kuberska * Teresa E. Gallion
Kimberly Burnham * Shareef Abdur – Rasheed
Ashok K. Bhargava * Elizabeth Castillo * Swapna Behera
Tezmin Ition Tsai * William S. Peters, Sr.

Now Available

www.innerchildpress.com/the-year-of-the-poet

and there is much, much more !

visit . . .

http://www.innerchildpress.com
/anthologies-sales-special.php

Also check out our Authors and
all the wonderful Books
Available at :

http://www.innerchildpress.com
/the-book-store.php

World Healing World Peace
PoEtRy
i am a believer!
www.worldhealingworldpeacepoetry.com
Coexist
Inner Child PRESS
Let Us Share Our Magic With You
www.innerchildpress.com

Now Available

www.worldhealingworldpeacepoetry.com

i support
World Healing
World Peace

www.worldhealingworldpeacepoetry.com

World Healing World Peace
PoEtRy
i am a believer !

World Healing World Peace 2018

Now Available

www.worldhealingworldpeacepoetry.com

Inner Child Press International

'building cultural bridges of understanding'

Meet the Board of Directors

William S. Peters, Sr.
Chair Person
Founder
Inner Child Enterprises
Inner Child Press

Hülya N Yılmaz
Director
Editing Services
Co-Chair Person

Nizar Sartawi
Director
International
Relations

Fahredin B. Shehu
Director
Cultural Affairs

Gail Weston Shazor
Director
Anthologies

Kimberly Burnham
Director
Cultural Ambassador
Pacific Northwest
USA

Deborah Smart
Director
Publicity
Marketing

De'Andre Hawthorne
Director
Performance Poetry

Ashok K. Bhargava
Director
WINAwards

www.innerchildpress.com

Inner Child Press International
'building bridges of cultural understanding'
Meet our Cultural Ambassadors
Fahredin Shehu
Director of Cultural
Faleha Hassan
Iraq ~ USA
Elizabeth E. Castillo
Philippines
Antoinette Coleman
Chicago
Midwest USA
Ananda Nepali
Nepal - Tibet
Northern India
Kimberly Burnham
Pacific Northwest
USA
Alicja Kuberska
Poland
Eastern Europe
Swapna Behera
India
Southeast Asia
Kolade O. Freedom
Nigeria
West Africa
Monsif Beroual
Morocco
Northern Africa
Ashok K. Bhargava
Canada
Tzemin Ition Tsai
Republic of China
Greater China
Alicia M. Ramírez
Mexico
Central America
Christena AV Williams
Jamaica
Caribbean
Aziz Mountassir
Morocco
Northern Africa
Shareef Abdur-Rasheed
Southeastern USA
Laure Charazac
France
Western Europe
Mohammad Ikbal Harb
Lebanon
Middle East
Mohamed Abdel
Aziz Shmeis
Egypt
Middle East
www.innerchildpress.com

This Anthological Publication
is underwritten solely by

Inner Child Press

Inner Child Press is a Publishing Company Founded and Operated by Writers. Our personal publishing experiences provides us an intimate understanding of the sometimes daunting challenges Writers, New and Seasoned may face in the Business of Publishing and Marketing their Creative "Written Work".

For more Information

Inner Child Press

www.innerchildpress.com

Inner Child Press International
'building bridges of cultural understanding'

~ *fini* ~

www.ingramcontent.com/pod-product-compliance
Lightning Source LLC
LaVergne TN
LVHW051050080426
835508LV00019B/1796

9781970020687